THRIVING

AS A SPECIAL EDUCATOR:

BALANCING YOUR PRACTICES AND IDEALS

JANE BURNETTE & CASSANDRA PETERS-JOHNSON, EDITORS

Council for Exceptional Children

1110 North Glebe Road, Suite 300
Arlington, VA 22201-5704
Phone: 703-620-3660
Toll free: 800-224-6830
TTY: 866-915-5000
www.cec.sped.org

Library of Congress Cataloging-in-Publication Data

This publication was supported by Contract No. ED-99-CO-0026 between the U.S. Department of Education and the Council for Exceptional Children. Any opinions, findings, conclusions, or recommendations expressed in this publication are those of the author(s) and do not necessarily reflect the view of the organizations or agencies that provided support for this project.

Acknowledgments

Content Focus Group:

We gratefully acknowledge the time and thoughtfulness of many special educators and CEC staff who agreed to participate in a focus group at the stage when the issues of concern to the book's audience were first being identified. These educators — Lee Hanson, Rebecca Marti, Debbi DeSantis, Wendy Welsh, Susan Bergert, Antonia Reynolds, Lynn Boyer, Cassandra Peters-Johnson, Abigail Miklos, Carol Pierce, Jennifer Miller, and Jane Burnette — shaped the content which our authors have addressed.

Chapter Authors:

This book could not have been produced without the years of wisdom represented by seasoned educators Lynn Boyer, Lynne Cook, Nancy K. French, Marilyn Friend, K. Sarah Hall, Cassandra Peters-Johnson, and Teresa Zutter, each of whom contributed a chapter or chapters on the topics in this volume. We thank these authors for their dedication to the field of special education and for sharing their expertise in the respective topics about which they have written.

Reviewers:

Two former CEC Teachers of the Year deserve recognition and appreciation for reviewing this book and providing their insights. They are Matty Rodriguez-Walling and Kelli Kercher.

Production Credits:

Jane Burnette, Editor, finalized the topics, coordinated contacts with the six authors, edited the manuscripts, chose the cover painting, and lovingly guided the book toward its final form.

Trudy Turner, contract monitor, patiently reviewed and assisted throughout the production of this manuscript.

Jan Swartzendruber, writer and designer, Editech Services, Inc., Reston, Virginia, designed the book and contributed to the final editorial process.

Cover Painting:

The painting on our cover, "The Juggler," is the work of Ms. Lucy Raverat. Her generosity in giving CEC permission to use the painting is gratefully acknowledged. Ms. Raverat's biography is found at the back of this book. We also wish to thank the distributor of her art, the Bridgeman Art Library (see bridgemanart.com) for its cooperation. A special thank you is owed to Mrs. Gerry Denning, proprietor of the Bowmoore Gallery, Wiltshire, England, who made arrangements with Ms. Raverat on our behalf.

We also appreciate Ms. Raverat's permission to allow us to use images based on her painting within the text of the book.

TABLE OF CONTENTS

Introduction:
About the Topic and Authors

LYNN BOYER
SENIOR DIRECTOR FOR PROGRAM DEVELOPMENT
COUNCIL FOR EXCEPTIONAL CHILDREN (CEC)

For many years, one of the Council for Exceptional Children's best sellers has been the *Survival Guide for the First-Year Special Education Teacher.* This guide has helped hundreds of new special education teachers anticipate and overcome the challenges of their first year in the classroom. With the chronic shortage of licensed special educators, though, the importance of supporting special educators beyond the first year is critical. Helping special educators to remain and thrive in their chosen field has emerged as the most important means of ensuring a highly qualified special educator supporting every student with a disability. This need was the impetus for *Thriving as a Special Educator: Balancing Your Practices and Ideals.*

The concept for the book started with a small group of special educators at CEC Headquarters talking about their own expectations of special education teaching and how they differed from the realities of the classroom. Eventually a focus group of CEC member teachers met to elaborate on those differences. Each of the teachers talked about what she had done to reconcile those differences with her commitment to the profession, confront the challenges, and create a set of expectations and practices that allowed her to remain in the profession and thrive.

As the book took shape, six authors were asked to write about accommodating the challenges of special education so that the commitment to teach children and youth with disabilities would not fade but flourish and allow the teacher to thrive. *Thriving as a Special Educator* brings strength from the experiences and knowledge of each of its authors. Each has a long history in special education, ranging from teacher to administrator, school psychologist, speech/language therapist, and teacher educator.

Meet the Authors

Chapter 1: Deciding ~ Once More ~ to Be a Special Educator

LYNN BOYER opens the book by asking you to consider why you became a special educator and how you decided to renew your commitment to the field. If your commitment is faltering, she begins the process of exploring what can be done to help you decide, once more, to be a special educator. Lynn is Senior Director for Program Development at the Council for Exceptional Children in Arlington, Virginia. When this book was being planned, she was directing the National Clearinghouse for Professions in Special Education at CEC. Her work in that federal project, and now in determining the course of publications for CEC, is rooted in her commitment to support new teachers through mentoring and induction programs and to provide professional development that helps them feel capable of meeting the challenges of the profession. Lynn's 20 years of experience as a school psychologist and special education administrator give her a broad understanding of the processes of special education, the development of services for children who are identified as needing special education, and, most importantly, the critical importance of having teachers who are committed and skilled to support children and youth with disabilities to achieve their academic and social goals.

Chapter 2: Working With Principals and Administrators: Developing Skills in Politics and Negotiation

TERESA ZUTTER uses her many years as a teacher of students with varied disabilities, as principal of a middle school serving students with emotional or behavioral disabilities, and now as Director of the Office of Alternative School Programs for Fairfax County Public Schools, Fairfax, Virginia, to give seasoned advice about how to navigate your entry into the teaching profession and remain there to thrive. In Chapter 2, Teresa's pragmatic tips will help you to develop a support system that cushions the hard days and allows you to develop as a professional who is valued in your school and prepared to contribute in the broader field of special education. While teaching students with disabilities in juvenile correctional facilities, Teresa received the Agnes Meyer Outstanding Teacher of the Year award in Fairfax County Public Schools, a high honor in the twelfth largest school district in the United States. She is the only special educator who has been honored in this way. Currently, Teresa prepares, mentors, and supervises teachers, helping them to thrive through her reality-based insight and generous and compassionate spirit. You will find her chapter an inspiration and a delight to read.

Chapter 3: Collaborating With Professionals and Parents Without Being Overwhelmed: Building Partnerships and Teams

LYNNE COOK is professor in the Department of Special Education at California State University, Northridge. Here, she co-authors two chapters that address difficult challenges that confront special educators. In Chapter 3, Lynne and co-author Marilyn Friend face head-on the circumstances in which collaboration is appropriate and necessary to ensure services to students. In Chapter 5, "Making Paperwork Work for You and Your Students," she and co-author Sarah Hall take up another difficult issue: the challenge of managing the administrative requirements and associated paperwork inherent in the field of special education. Lynne is well known in the special education field for her research into teacher satisfaction and teacher retention. She understands deeply the intricate challenges of special education and the impact they have on a teacher's commitment to remain in the field and to thrive. Lynne's longstanding work in preparing special educators and working with school districts gives her a unique perspective on the results of teacher preparation and the importance of continuing support for teachers. Such a perspective brings to her chapters practical advice and suggestions that are grounded in reality.

MARILYN FRIEND is professor and Chairperson of the Department of Specialized Education Services at the University of North Carolina–Greensboro. She has published widely on the topic of collaboration and consultation. In Chapter 3 she writes with her frequent co-author Lynne Cook about "Collaborating With Professionals and Parents Without Being Overwhelmed." Marilyn has spent over 25 years teaching students in public schools and preparing teachers for the challenges of special education. She has shepherded and studied special education teachers as they moved out of self-contained classrooms into instructional leadership roles that include collaborating with all professionals delivering services to students with disabilities; co-teaching with general education and special education teachers; and assuming a strong role in advocating — in schools and with parents — the inclusion of students with disabilities in general education classrooms. In her easy-to-read style, she reinforces the necessity of refining and embracing your collaboration skills to make them an integral part of your success as a special educator. Marilyn and Lynne have filled Chapter 3 with specific advice and cautions that will help you navigate the sometimes perilous field of collaboration and turn it into a means for thriving in your profession.

Chapter 4: Maximizing the Services of Paraeducators

NANCY K. FRENCH is associate research professor at the University of Colorado at Denver and Director of The PAR2A Center, which offers training for teachers and administrators in the supervision of paraeducators and training and career information for paraeducators. Nancy writes on a subject that she lives each day and researches continuously. She guides you in accepting the support that a paraeducator can bring to your teaching while you define and maintain your role as the instructional leader in this special relationship. Nancy helps you to project your role as leader beyond the first year of teaching into those subsequent years when you are confident in your teaching and thriving in your profession. Her chapter provides a spotlight on an area in which special educators are almost never trained: how to clarify the roles of professionals and paraeducators and establish this vital relationship. Nancy is uniquely able to address this subject because of her extensive experience in training teachers and her deep knowledge of the dynamics of teacher-paraeducator relationships. Her chapter will bring you the insight you need to invigorate this aspect of your profession.

Chapter 5: Making Paperwork Work for You and Your Students

K. SARAH HALL is an associate professor in the Department of Special Education at California State University, Northridge. During the 2003–2004 school year, she took a leave of absence to teach children K-5 with learning disabilities. In Chapter 5, she and co-author Lynne Cook tackle a difficult challenge for special educators — accommodating the administrative demands associated with paperwork. They identify the actual demands required by federal and local laws and point out that paperwork is often a generic term for any demand that special educators feel interrupts their actual teaching time in the classroom. In addition, Sarah and Lynne describe straightforward and practical ways to make paperwork part of classroom activities; so that, with advance planning, paperwork actually saves you time by doubling as a teaching and communication tool. Chapter 5 will help you to reconstruct your perspective on paperwork and moderate any impact it is having on your flourishing in your chosen profession.

Chapter 6: The View from the Top of the Mountain

CASSANDRA PETERS-JOHNSON directs the special education-related services professionals in the District of Columbia Public Schools. During the time that this book was planned, she was Assistant Executive Director for Professional Development at the Council for Exceptional Children, overseeing the development of all publications and products of CEC. Cassandra brings experience in special education administration and a career long commitment to the needs of children and youth with speech and hearing and communication disorders. In the final chapter to the book, Cassandra takes you outside your daily work to the opportunities that thriving special educators use to enhance their professional skills, increase their confidence, and build broader networks with other special educators. She offers a perspective from the pinnacle you may be striving for: the view from the top of the mountain. In her words, this is the point where you experience the satisfaction of thriving and reap the rewards of a career in which "you are truly making a difference to your student, to our culture and society, and to the future."

**Chapter
1**

Deciding ~ Once More ~ to Be a Special Educator

LYNN BOYER

SENIOR DIRECTOR FOR PROGRAM DEVELOPMENT
COUNCIL FOR EXCEPTIONAL CHILDREN

Thriving. It's a word that conjures up momentum, satisfaction, accomplishment, prospering. Many of us as special educators are thriving. Our chosen profession has proven to be a good match with our skills, interests, and passions. We have maintained our personal integrity and belief structure. We have reconciled our expectations with reality. We are assuming a greater role within our profession, and we see that the children are achieving. This experience of growing and flourishing and finding fulfillment has not come easily, though; for special education is a profession of unique challenges and not for the faint of heart!

In this chapter we will consider why you chose special education as a career, whether your expectations met the realities of your classroom and school, questions to consider in taking a measure of whether you are thriving, and steps to take if you feel your commitment is fading.

A Choice That Matters

When you chose to be a special educator, you made a **profound decision.** You accepted humanity's obligation to assist those who are especially challenged, through no fault of their own, and honored your own personal need to contribute actively to the growth of young people.

> ~ Choosing to be a special educator is often an **unanticipated decision.** It may have happened for you as you helped your brother or sister finally learn to use a spoon or as you watched the delight of a child with autism participate in games at a summer camp.

> ~ Choosing to be a special educator is always a **bold decision.** Student progress is not rapid. Other teachers often lack appreciation for the work. Parents' anger, guilt, frustration, and confusion can mark your relationship with them.

With our students' welfare at stake, we have an obligation to do all we can to thrive.

> ~ Choosing to be a special educator can be a **tenuous decision,** as well, one that must constantly be nurtured, respected, reflected upon, re-invigorated, and honored. Approximately 9% of American students have special education teachers: Those students deserve teachers who remain committed to their decision and are thriving in their chosen profession. With our students' welfare at stake, we have an obligation to do all we can to thrive.

What Does the Research Tell Us?

Research in our field demonstrates the impact of the difficulties and challenges of teaching special education. The Survey of Personnel Needs in Special Education, a federal study of the special education workforce, revealed that during 1999–2000, school districts had 69,000 special education openings (U.S. Department of Education, 2002). These openings included new positions created because of increases in the special education population. But they also included vacancies created by special educators who left education entirely, switched from our field to general education or other education professions, or retired. Every year, approximately 6% of the special education workforce leave education altogether, while another 7.4 % transfer to general education (Boe, Bobbitt, Cook, & Barkanic, 1998).

Why does that happen? What occurs in schools to cause persons committed to the education of students with disabilities to turn their backs on those students and the profession? What disillusionment, frustration, anger, and guilt do these teachers experience when they realize that what they thought was a good match with their beliefs, interest, and skills was, in fact, all wrong? What kept them from thriving? Most importantly, what did they need to know and do to thrive and remain as committed professionals?

Why Did You Become a Special Educator?

Try to remember the first time you said, "I'm going to be a special educator." Did you say it to one of your parents, to a college professor, to a friend? If the response was, "Why?", what did you answer? Were you able to describe clearly the values that made this challenging profession so appealing to you? Did you understand the beliefs that often interact unconsciously in persons who choose to teach children with unique learning needs?

With the luxury of hindsight, you probably know now that your decision reflected deeply held beliefs that

- education is a right and a privilege for all;

- each individual has value and merits respect;

- schools shape our society; and

- learning is lifelong.

A belief structure that encompasses these values is fundamental to teaching students with disabilities. Persons who say to themselves or to another, "I'm going to be a special educator," have acquired or developed through family, personal, or other work experiences a belief structure that encompasses these values. This belief structure allows the teacher to be an advocate for children with learning challenges, a tireless communicator with families, a creative seeker of resources, a determined ally with other teachers and community members, and a master of uncommon ways to make learning possible for students.

With such a compelling belief structure, those preparing to be special educators and teachers in their first or second year with students often maintain expectations that all educators will act in ways that reflect these beliefs. They also expect that schools will operate daily with these fundamental tenets driving decisions and that the students receiving special education services will be diligent in working with the teacher to reach their own educational goals. When reality does not match expectations, thriving is hard; and vital energy is used to reconcile the conditions of work each day.

Put down this book for a few minutes, and try this exercise in introspection. Make a cup of coffee, walk around the block, or play some quiet music. As you relax, think about your choice to be a special educator and about what you expected your first year of teaching to be like. What kind of relationship did you expect to have with your principal? How did you expect services to be provided to children with disabilities? What role did you expect to have within the faculty? How did you envision the reception you and your students would have in other classrooms? What did you think your classroom would look like? What resources did you expect would be available for instruction? As you reflect, consider this: Did you find what you expected? Did you ever question your decision to be a special educator?

As you reflect, consider this: Did you find what you expected? Did you ever question your decision to be a special educator?

Ours Is a Complicated Profession

Special educators must deal continuously with the administrative aspect of their job, which is huge.

The reality of special education now includes focused collaboration with all persons implementing an individualized education program (IEP), support to general education teachers, and services to students within the general education classroom. In addition, as a result of the Individuals With Disabilities Education Act (IDEA), as reauthorized in 1997, all teachers for students with disabilities are expected to provide instruction grounded in the general education curriculum and advocate inclusion of their students in state assessments. Bottom line: Special education teachers who entered the field expecting and wanting to be in classrooms of their own may now find themselves working in many different general education classrooms in order to instruct students on their caseloads. This could mean learning to team teach and devoting extra hours to acquire greater depth in general education curriculum content. On the other hand, a special educator must also learn to provide leadership to paraeducators, who often will end up doing the work they as teachers expected to do: teaching reading comprehension and decoding, assisting students to edit written work, showing students how to think through the steps in a math problem, and so on. Finally, special educators deal continuously with the administrative aspect of their job, which is huge. Its enormous impact on teaching time and personal time wasn't part of university training and licensure: Teachers only learn it — sink-or-swim — through on-the-job experience.

Special educators often find, as well, that their principals have limited awareness of the potential achievements of students with disabilities. Principals who lack this sensitivity may provide only minimal administrative support to the teacher personally and within the faculty. This can hamper a special educator's efforts to include students with disabilities in general classrooms and to be respected within the faculty as a valued colleague. When the realities of the profession are coupled with conditions in a school that do not match expectations, the early months and years of teaching are both a challenge and a test of one's commitment.

The Early Years Are Hard Years

The literature on teacher attrition reveals that, during the first year with their own students, teachers demonstrate a predictable but difficult and complex evolution to professional competence. They begin with great anticipation, excited to be taking their place in a classroom. Shortly, however, their idealism and high energy are assaulted by the reality of the skill and effort required to meet the needs of children and the daily demands of the profession. They enter what is often called a survival stage where they are preoccupied with their adequacy as a teacher and control of the classroom. This precipitates a downward curve of disillusionment that continues until early February, when a period of rejuvenation begins. This period continues its ascent throughout the spring as the new teacher reflects on the challenges that were faced and overcome and anticipates the conclusion of the year.

The ease with which teachers resolve this assault of reality early in their careers and begin to thrive, maintaining positive momentum toward career satisfaction, results from several factors. They include

    (a) the accumulation of practical knowledge;

    (b) the teacher's own personality including the willingness to seek help;

    (c) the manner in which expectations were reconciled with reality; and

    (d) the teacher's capacity to reflect on personal and professional growth.

What Does This Mean for You?

Go back to our earlier exercises — remembering when you first decided to become a special educator and what you expected. How did those dreams and expectations compare with your professional life now? If your examination revealed that your reality as a special educator is greatly different from what you expected, there are important questions to consider so you can proceed and thrive in the profession:

    ~ What about your profession does give you satisfaction?

    ~ Where are the sources of conflict and tension in your professional role?

    ~ Is your value system still fundamental in the choices you make each day for yourself and your students?

    ~ Are you willing to identify resources and supports that could enhance your ability to thrive, and then use them?

This reflection on your choice and expectations through the lens of experience brings with it the humbling task of admitting mistakes, recognizing persistent characteristics of human nature, and understanding and accepting the political nature of school districts and schools. It also calls upon you to appraise your personal knowledge and skills, acknowledge the pressures on you to change, and identify and admit to those conditions over which you have no control.

This reflection calls upon you to appraise your skills, face pressures to change, and admit to those conditions over which you have no control.

This process of reexamining expectations carries with it, however, the opportunity to think flexibly, reorient your actions, consider the availability of resources, and emerge from the process recommitted from a perspective of reality and insight. This may reveal to you the need for personal changes in the ways you accomplish your work or seek resources. It may bring you to accept new roles in your school and profession. You could become an advocator of change through committees, professional organizations, and enhanced affiliations with parents or other teachers. You may contribute what you have learned through writing and publishing. You may feel impelled to exert your influence as a leader through political processes. Taking action for change — no matter the routes you choose — creates energy of its own, which is then available to you for growing and thriving. This self-examination process can invigorate you and crystallize for you the steps necessary to accomplish your goals and help your students to accomplish theirs.

Recommitting to the Profession

As you consider the questions in this chapter, you may realize that over the years you have developed an even stronger commitment to the profession than you had initially. This renewed commitment is stronger because it is made with an understanding of the demands of the profession, the environments in which it is practiced, the ongoing need to replenish yourself through continuous learning, the value of engaging actively in your profession, the necessity to act as a change agent when necessary, and the importance of always modeling your belief structure. All these help you thrive as a special educator.

In the chapters that follow, special educators with specific expertise will offer resources, practical information, and new perspectives on old problems. We hope that you will find here insights and new ideas that will help you continue or begin to thrive in your chosen profession. A principal shares the importance of building a support network, creating win-win situations, communicating in ways that get your needs met, and being your own public relations advocate. Teacher educators offer strategies for collaborating with parents and other teachers without being overwhelmed, developing a relationship with paraeducators that supports you and the students, and using documentation requirements to your best advantage. In every chapter, you will find the authors describing activities and responsibilities that allow for personal growth and enhance the sense of thriving in the profession.

Thriving Is Important!

It is in your best interest to continuously reflect upon your choice of career to be sure it is meeting your values, needs, interests, and motivations.

Choosing special education as a career is a series of decisions. It is in your best interest and crucial to the outcomes for your students that you continuously evaluate and reflect upon your choice to be sure it is meeting your personal values, needs, interests, and motivations (Sarason, 1993). In this way, the decision is made — not just once but many times — to be committed to children and youth with disabilities and to thrive as you do so.

When you are thriving

- the satisfactions of your work outweigh the frustrations and disappointments;

- the belief structure that underlies your work remains a strong driving force for instruction;

- you are working with your students' families in partnerships that are child-focused;

- you experience professional growth through expanded relationships and involvement in the profession; and

- your students are growing and prospering academically and socially.

Children who are taught by committed and thriving special educators are fortunate. They have teachers who came to the field of special education because of a deep caring for their futures and stayed to teach them because they prefer the individual nature of special education, want the opportunity to work closely with each child, and accept the responsibility of primary impact.

A special educator thrives when personal values, needs, interests, and motivations are in accord with the responsibilities, challenges, and opportunities faced each day. In the end, however, a special educator knows the choice continues to be the right one when the children are thriving. A new but thriving special educator said it best: "This is where my heart is. This is my career. I enjoy what I do because of the type of child I work with — it's the children that keep me here."

You will know that you are thriving when your students are growing and prospering academically and socially.

References

Boe, E. E., Bobbitt, S. A., Cook, L. H., & Barkanic, G. (1998). *National trends in teacher supply and turnover for special and general education.* (Data Analysis Report No. 1998-DAR1). Philadelphia: University of Pennsylvania, Center for Research and Evaluation in Social Policy. (ERIC Document Reproduction Service No. ED 426 549).

Sarason, S. B. (1993). *You are thinking of teaching? Opportunities, problems, realities.* San Francisco: Jossey-Bass.

U.S. Department of Education. (2002). *Survey of personnel needs in special education.* Retrieved November 3, 2002, from http://www.spense.org

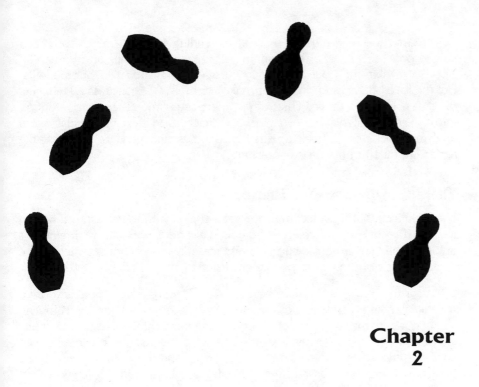

**Chapter
2**

Working With Principals and Administrators: Developing Skills in Politics and Negotiation

TERESA ZUTTER
FAIRFAX COUNTY PUBLIC SCHOOLS, FAIRFAX, VIRGINIA

Most teachers begin their careers with lofty goals of reaching kids' hearts and inspiring their minds to greatness. They want to lead their school to high achievement and listen to parents say such affirmations as, "If it weren't for this teacher, who knows where my child would be today?"

Inspired by Our Dreams

Teachers today, especially those in special education, have to possess tremendous conviction, passion, and perseverance to work effectively with children who require more from them than in times past. If teachers don't have these dreams, if they don't *really believe* they can make a significant difference in the lives of their students, then they shouldn't be teaching in the first place. It is as simple as that.

Master teaching requires a creative blending of heart, mind, body, and soul in order to produce that winning combination of skills and humanity. This is how we bring out the best in ourselves and offer it to our students. But the love of teaching isn't what makes or breaks our success as teachers or what helps us to thrive. The truth is, there are many other factors that go into the school scene that can persuade teachers to nest in the classroom until retirement or to pack up their belongings and head to the next big adventure far from the halls of learning.

There Be Dragons Out There!

I have noticed that most teachers are preoccupied with the classroom setting itself for the first several years — how they will get along with their students and how they will organize curricula and materials to anchor learning in the restless minds of the young people entrusted to them.

But the reality is, there is far more to the story if your goal is to be a truly outstanding educator over the next 30 years or so of your life. Knowing what your administrator expects from you in your professional performance is just as important as being aware of students' needs. Failure to acknowledge the importance of this crucial relationship and the expectations placed on you can lead to increased stress and fatigue right at a time when you need supreme confidence and boundless energy.

Just as early explorers in the 15th century read sea charts that noted, "Beyond this point, there be dragons!", it is also important to recognize that sometimes there are dragons in the world of teaching that can swamp your boat. They come in many varieties, and identifying them early in your career will help you avoid becoming overwhelmed and burned-out in your new profession. Many of these dragons, such as apathy, disheartenment, and negativity, can creep up over the years; and, before you know it, they have thrown you off course from your original destination.

This chapter will attempt to suggest a plan of action that describes the dragons and how to escape them in order to help you navigate safe passage in unknown, and sometimes treacherous, waters.

Just What Does My Principal Expect?

If school administrators could speak freely about what they most desire to see in their staff members, I think most of them would generate a similar list of attributes and behaviors. You would not have been offered a contract if you had not been perceived as having the necessary skills and the knowledge to do the job well. Obviously, school administrators also want to see your true commitment as demonstrated by dependability, punctuality, initiative, and responsibility. Observing consistent, proper, and attractive attire, seeing your good posture, and even hearing a pleasant tone of voice coming out of your classroom can go a long way to ease the mind of a busy administrator.

But beyond these obvious signs of professionalism, administrators want to know that they can expect you to show good judgment, common sense, and tactful communication with everyone with whom you interact. They want to know that you "can work and play nicely with others"! Remember that many school settings are very much like families, and you are still integrating into that family. The last thing an administrator wants to do is mop up some "interpersonal mess" on the school staff.

Yes, Everyone IS Still Watching You!

Like it or not, the importance of first impressions cannot be overstated when joining any new organization. Educators are astute observers of behaviors, and for better or for worse, they will continue to check you out as one of the newer members of the team. To make matters even more nerve-racking, your administrator will also be watching over time to see how well his or her judgment in hiring you plays out in the real school setting.

It is normal to be self-conscious and to feel a degree of uncertainty for the first several years. During this time, following certain unspoken rules may smooth the way as you find your niche. Acknowledge the obvious, sit back, relax, and smile. Follow the ten pointers below, and you'll be just fine!

Certain unspoken "rules" may smooth the way as you find your niche.

POINTER ONE: LOOK THE PART, ACT THE PART

The transition from college life or another career into teaching can actually be an exciting and enjoyable experience. Your administrator and fellow teachers know that the way you look, act, and speak has a direct connection to how the students and community perceive the school as a whole. It is imperative not to embarrass your colleagues who have worked long and hard to present a professional image.

Unlike many other professional environments, teachers have the luxury of being able to dress well and still express their individuality in comfort. Hair styles, clothing, and footwear can all be adapted for the reality of classroom life. Since few other professionals have dozens of pairs of eyes watching their every move for a minimum of seven hours a day, it is important for teachers to remember that there is a fine line between being comfortable and being a fashion nightmare.

Observe the style of attire worn by your administrator and other staff members, and attempt to follow a certain reasonable protocol in order to facilitate acceptance into the school community. As your confidence and skills increase, keep in mind that this is no time to let down the standards in your personal appearance. Remind yourself of what you chose to wear to that first interview years before, and compare that outfit to how you look each day. If you look like you just threw on what was closest to the bed as you raced to work, it is hard to expect others to take you seriously. *People will invest in you to the degree that you invest in yourself.*

POINTER TWO: YOU CAN'T DO IT ALONE

Regardless of what area of special education you have chosen, it is a field of work that, on some days, can be full of tremendous joy, satisfaction, excitement, and love. Other days are replete with challenge, frustration, despair, and disappointment. It comes as quite a shock for new special educators to learn that not everyone always thinks as highly of the field as one might expect. Other teachers on the faculty can sometimes focus on the low student/teacher ratio and ignore or be unaware of the especially difficult requirements of your job. Inclusion strategies can also have a controversial impact. Some special education teachers team-teach or serve two or more schools. This scheduling arrangement is not always well understood or appreciated by other teachers. Some teachers on the staff may feel ill-prepared to work with students with certain disabilities and may resent the expectations placed on them to serve a diverse group of students who often require special accommodations.

If you really want to make it as a thriving lifer, sooner or later you will need a shoulder to cry on or a comrade to confide in.

With so many possible stumbling blocks, some special educators gallop in like the Lone Ranger to save the day for their chosen students, only to find that, as time goes by, there is very little fanfare and they get virtually no pats on the back. If you really want to make it into the category of a thriving lifer, sooner or later you will need a shoulder to cry on or a comrade to confide in. This is the critical moment. Picking that person — or a select few persons — *very carefully* makes all the difference. If you make the wrong choice, your reputation can be dragged into the mud with other staff members known for their negativity and misery. If you choose correctly, you will have friends and mentors quite possibly for the duration of your career.

The next logical question might be, "How do I attract the right support advocates?" Most teaching veterans are not overly impressed with teachers who come in like gangbusters. It is wonderful to be full of ideas and confidence, but in the novice stage it is far more appealing to others to watch your gifts and talents unfold subtly over time. This is not a time to try to impress them with your knowledge and latest techniques. Time and experience weigh in heavily on how your contributions will be accepted. Instead, watch, listen, and learn from the quiet veterans who "whistle while they work."

Veteran master teachers are rarely boisterous, overbearing, or grandstanding in nature. They go about their work with quiet joy. They have passed the critical tests of time that filtered out other teachers whose primary purpose was aimed at recognition and status. Typically, these old-timers have extensive experience on numerous committees and initiatives; each one can be a fountain of knowledge, history, and wisdom if you are wise enough to take the time to learn from them. As I said before, they are also watching you. They are looking for your maturity, common sense, and social grace. They want to be sure you are not just another flash in the pan for the first 2 or 3 years, but rather that you are someone to whom it is worth devoting their time and effort for the sake of the continued growth of the faculty's value. You can bet they are checking in with your administrator to offer feedback on your integration into the school culture. Choose your cohorts carefully, and make it count.

Just how do you avoid the negative naysayers who want to suck you into the black hole of hopeless acrimony? On any staff of any school there will always be at least one person or a little group of disgruntled persons that always has an axe to grind, an issue to grouse, or a wrong to rail against. They put all the passion they should devote to the love of students into this selected cause; and, as a result, they can make life miserable for countless colleagues and administrators as they try to further the righteousness of their mission. When all is said and done, their behavior brings down others around them, it distracts teachers from their primary duties, and it annoys administrators, who are forced to spend their precious time dealing with demands that refuse easy resolution. These people are never happy and, in all probability, never will be happy. Even if the school or school system addresses the alleged wrongdoing, the zealot will be quick to pick up the next cause and battle on.

Cliques of negative people are always on the lookout for new members. Avoid these people at all costs, especially if you are fairly new and impressionable. At this stage, all new information carries fairly even weight, and the arguments can at first seem reasonable and worthy. But in the long haul, your reputation in the eyes of your administrator will sour as surely as the lemon drops you ate as a child. How do you find the balance? It is still pretty simple. Hear out everyone with genuine diplomacy. Recognize that in all probability, every teacher's heart is in the right place some or most of the time. Smile frequently, and try to relax with all the members of your school staff. Teachers with dark intent will eventually give up recruitment overtures if you pull away from association with certain behaviors — including tantrums — with kind yet firm non-engagement. Trust your instincts, line yourself up with winners, and enjoy the company of those colleagues who, at the end of a long day, refresh you with hope and inspiration. You and your administrator will both be able to breathe easier.

Trust your instincts, line yourself up with winners, and enjoy the company of those colleagues who, at the end of a long day, refresh you with hope and inspiration.

POINTER THREE: HONOR TIME

As you strive to make a good impression, get along with all of the faculty, come across to everyone professionally, and — oh, yes — also *teach those kids* in front of you, you will soon have an opportunity to converse with your building administrator. And, yes, there are rules to follow on this interaction as well. Begin with the knowledge that every administrator is unbelievably busy, never has enough time to mark off all items on the daily list of to dos, and usually misses the family waiting at home far more than ever can be mentioned. In light of this, there are some background facts that must be kept in mind when the big moment comes to have a conversation.

Often, teachers will want to visit with their principal at the end of a long, hard day. Some teachers have little recognition that, although they will soon head out to the parking lot, the administrator's day is hardly over.

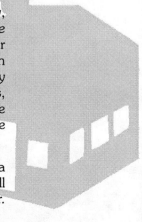

Suspension calls, parent conferences, teacher evaluations, and forms and surveys — all due yesterday — await the principal before the closing bell. Good administrators do care about their staff and students and often work 50 to 60 hours a week, including the sneak visit into the office on weekends when it is quiet and work can be done without interruption. There are ways to bring your administrator's attention to both easy and difficult issues that will endear to your boss throughout your career.

State clearly what is happening, and come prepared to suggest some possible solutions.

First, Be Brief and to the Point. State clearly what is happening; if it is an identified problem, come prepared to suggest some possible solutions. Do not lay the dilemma at the feet of your administrator and walk away as he or she is left to figure out what to do next. If the problem is well known, ask others on the staff what might help the situation, and offer to share these thoughts as you and the administrator brainstorm together.

Second, If the News Is Good, Affirm the Administrator. State that you, the staff, and the students are grateful for the obvious support the administrator has lent to the process, even when that support is behind the scenes and unknown to others. Administrators are not out there looking for accolades, but they do like to know that their efforts are acknowledged and appreciated. Much of what they do in a day's time can be difficult and tedious, and it doesn't cost a thing to share the good moments together. Most people have limited awareness of the dozens of activities accomplished by administrators, usually because administrators are too busy to talk about it!

Third, Remember That Timing Is Everything. Maintain sensitivity to the other demands competing for the administrator's time and attention. As you come in, ask if this is still a good time to meet. If the administrator just received an urgent call requiring action, it is unlikely you will receive the full attention you deserve, no matter how concerned your principal is for your well-being. Get to know the principal's secretary or administrative assistant, and find out the status of the day before you walk in. The secretary will inevitably know the best time to schedule an appointment and will suggest times when hearing "yes" to your proposals is most likely.

Fourth, End the Meeting on a Positive Note. Regardless of the content of the conversation, let the administrator know that you appreciate the time devoted to discussing the topic and you look forward to being able to speak again soon. Principals are no different than any one else. They are drawn to people who make their lives easier and more pleasant, and they avoid those who pose only quandaries and quarrels.

POINTER FOUR: RESIST THE URGE TO HOST A PITY PARTY

Whining and complaining usually start out with a slow wind-up. At first, concerns may seem reasonable and worthy of attention. But, as they say, it is all in the delivery. Your administrator will stay open to your issue more willingly if you modulate your voice, avoid histrionics, and *if at all possible, do not cry*. Once the tears start flowing, attention is drawn away from the problem and is immediately enlisted to herd emotions back under control. Many adults, both male and female, are uncomfortable watching another adult lose it, and resentment for having to engage in a more personal manner than desired can cause the administrator to tune out the original situation that started it all. While an occasional incident will hardly cause irreversible damage, repeated experiences with the "woe is me" routine wears out even the most compassionate boss. If you see your administrator suddenly reverse course when he or she sees you coming down the hall, you can pretty much surmise that you may have taken the show one step too far. *Beware of this melodramatic dragon!*

POINTER FIVE: PRESENT YOURSELF AS A GENUINE ASSET

Whether they admit it or not, most administrators like it when you can look at issues from their point of view. They often sit at the helm of a very complex social entity, namely a school, and wonder if anyone out there realizes just how complicated situations can get at times. You will surely win a smile from your principal if you openly tell him or her that you want to be a valuable, contributing, and dependable team member who can be counted on by everyone in the school. If you make it one of your goals to always attempt to be part of the solution and rarely, if ever, an irritant to anyone's day, then chances are good that you will be sought out to sit on important steering committees and advisory groups where real change occurs. Let the administrator know that you realize all worthwhile endeavors take time, effort, and sometimes, pure doggedness. You are there to help, not to get in the way. It is music to the administrator's ears to hear that you are available to assist on laborious or time-consuming projects. Whenever you offer a gift of time, your value goes up several notches.

POINTER SIX: NEVER BASH THE BOSS

It appears that in any organization, it just seems inevitable that the opportunity to bad mouth the boss comes up eventually. It seems it can hardly be avoided, even when the boss is well liked and respected. So why does it happen over and over again? Who knows? There are probably lots of reasons. But our concern here is to reiterate the rule: Never bash the boss.

Administrators have a saying: School walls have ears. And is that ever true! Teachers who think they are confiding their innermost feelings in the sanctity of the teacher's lounge quickly find out how fast that information is mysteriously spread all the way to the doors of the main office before the day is out. If you are having problems, or if you feel you have a legitimate complaint, discuss it within the confines of trustworthy relationships that you have fostered with great care. If you can't find ways to resolve the concern on your own, then schedule an appointment to calmly and maturely discuss the matter with the administrator. Resorting to name-calling or inflammatory exaggerations will do nothing but antagonize the authority figure who might have been of greatest help.

It appears that in any organization, it just seems inevitable that the opportunity to bad mouth the boss comes up eventually.

Establish a Close-Knit Support Network Within Your School Before Branching Out to the Larger Community. You will need the ongoing support of this network to offer you sound advice, comfort, and strategies to further enhance your teaching skills. Subtlety and timing are critical as you advance yourself more into the mainstream of your school's initiatives and projects — and beyond.

POINTER 7: LISTEN, LISTEN, LISTEN . . . <u>THEN</u> VOLUNTEER

No one likes an upstart. No one likes a know-it-all. And no one likes someone who promises the world but fails to deliver. Even so, the next step to your growth as an important contributor in your school and in the surrounding community is to start attending open meetings that are of genuine interest to you. Start learning all you can about where the groups of interest to you are heading. Start piecing together the quilt of common goals. These will become more apparent as time goes by. It will be evident that although everyone is working toward an end product, the reasons that led each person to be a part of the group may be varied and extremely important to note.

You are still finding your niche in a community that is already well established. The hierarchy may be unspoken, but it is not completely invisible. Watch carefully, and you will discover who carries social and political power, who negotiates and mediates, and who waits for instructions and dutifully complies with requests. Tuck away this information, and then look for gaps where your strengths and talents can be put to best use.

You can float ideas suggesting ways you may be able to help, but wait for concrete requests for your assistance on specific tasks.

You can float ideas suggesting ways you may be able to help, but wait for concrete requests for your assistance on specific tasks. When you sign up for a project, treat it as seriously as the school plan. Do necessary research, create and disseminate concise and clear information, and deliver reports if and when asked — and deliver your information on time. Do not, under any circumstance, be the stumbling block holding up the group. Once you have established yourself as a dependable and meticulous coworker, you will find that avenues open up that allow you to become a well-respected and sought out main player. The art of the game, "You scratch my back, and I'll scratch yours," can become a fun and productive way to get mutual needs met with minimum effort and maximum benefit. Once you have been welcomed into the club, so to speak, you can expect to have access to the expertise of others who have until this time held off their familiarity.

When it is time for you to request a particular event or endeavor, you will be in an optimal position to have that idea welcomed openly. Recognize that everyone owns a piece of the action: students, parents, teacher colleagues, clinical staff, support staff, and administration. Keep requested tasks do-able and enjoyable, then allow everyone to receive credit for a job well done.

As Your Role Develops in the Community, Keep Your Boss Informed. Before taking another step, make a promise to yourself that you will apply

Pointer Eight not only to your next endeavor but also to all of your contacts outside of your school building. And what is Pointer Eight?

POINTER 8: TELL YOUR BOSS! TELL YOUR BOSS! TELL YOUR BOSS!

Administrators hate to be caught by surprise. Fielding a phone call from a community resident, local politician, or university contact goes so much more smoothly if the administrator can honestly say that he or she has been apprised of a project, publication, or special event in which the school's teachers have been involved. This does not mean you must receive permission *per se* for activities on your personal time, but it does indicate that you are keeping key persons with a need to know informed of your initiatives. In this way, the administrator can be helpful by offering advice on ways to proceed, or can offer a historical perspective on issues to avoid or when to use caution.

It is important that you are clear about what you need before you proceed. Make a list of specific desired activities or items to facilitate improvement to your classroom or school. No one can help effectively if you are unable to articulate your needs clearly and realistically. If you need mentors, say so. If you need landscaping plants or supplemental reading materials, specify exactly what you need. Many people who want to help "know someone who knows someone" who has access to what you want. Keep your requests reasonable and your conversations concise, genuine, and warm. Even if a person or company cannot give an abundance of time or material goods at a given time, if they feel appreciated for any gift, large or small, they will be more willing to return again and again to lend support to your various causes.

> **If donors feel appreciated for any gift, large or small, they will be more willing to return again and again to lend support to your various causes.**

The next step to building community support is to first find out who is out there. Locate and research businesses, organizations, and clubs that care about education and that place emphasis on various aspects of special education and special services. Many school districts maintain an office of community relations and business partnerships that can offer tremendous guidance. Most community organizations want to be helpful, but they need to know about specific activities that augment what is already being done in your school. One way to engage the community is to attend public meetings. If it is possible to be allowed to present a short explanation of your program or projects and offer ways that community members can become more involved, the outcome can be quite beneficial to both the group and to the students for whom you are seeking assistance.

Although the reality is that many projects are in need of financial support, it is critical to never turn down free help. Any investment of time and personal involvement with your students or school can later blossom into even more fruitful endeavors that can make a significant impact on a larger group of students. Welcome any and all overtures to be available to your school, and publicly acknowledge these individuals and the organization at large at every opportunity.

Stay Involved With Universities. Most new special educators fresh out of college already have links to known university faculty that can be maintained for years. It is not unusual for university education faculty to network with colleagues at other campuses as well. Even career switchers often need to enroll in coursework at a local campus to fulfill certification and endorsement requirements. As a result, teachers have numerous opportunities to meet professors who can assist with further contacts. All universities have a priority target to conduct research. Well-founded research opportunities in actual school environments are often sought, since the outcomes from real-life settings can be more easily generalized than artificial lab experiments.

Without fail, keep your administrator involved and knowledgeable at every step of the project.

University project managers are usually more than willing to work closely with local school districts and may offer wonderful support to the project. As an educator, you may find numerous ways to assist these efforts while receiving professional advice and assistance. Keep in mind that if students are involved, virtually all school districts have a human research committee that must review and approve projects prior to implementation. Without fail, keep your administrator involved and knowledgeable at every step of the project. Nothing should go on in a school that the principal is not completely aware of and approves.

In order to become the professional with whom the university loves to work, it is important to remain accessible, engaged, and available for follow-up. Maintain frequent and clear communication. Be honest about limitations and system constraints. If any particular aspect of the project might possibly conflict with your school system's regulations, policies, or procedures, discuss it early, and adapt the project as necessary prior to implementation. It is frustrating to university personnel to invest in labor intensive up-front work, including grant proposals and data documentation, only to have the school contact suddenly disappear from the scene. Negotiate a set period of time that you can confidently contract, and then make every effort to fulfill all obligations to both the students and the university investigators.

Finally, be sure to give credit where credit is due. Professors are under enormous pressure to produce and publish results. Every research endeavor should be presented in such a way that it enhances the reputation of both the school system and the university departments.

Analyze District Political Processes at Work. School districts are under scrutiny in ways that have financial repercussions. Emphasis on standardized test scores, school reports, and accreditation requirements have increased the impact of decisions. School boards and administrative leadership team members are subject to pressures, limitations, and financial parameters that affect these decisions; and it is important to remain sensitive to these constraints. This awareness extends to your principal as well. For example, if a decision has been made to cut materials and supplies by 5%, clearly it would be unwise to approach your principal with a request for an expensive software program or enrichment kits.

Here are some tips to help you stay knowledgeable of the financial and political climate:

- Read what your administrator reads. Ask for resources that he or she finds informative and accurate in predicting trends and current issues. Many administrators are willing to share professional journals, articles, and favorite authors if they know these materials will actually be read and appreciated.

- Attend public forums. What you hear and see will have a definite impact on how you approach future projects.

- Study longitudinal reports on local and state needs. Offer to represent your district on state committees and advisory groups. Your administrator can feel a sense of pride if you come across as an articulate and knowledgeable ambassador of the school.

- Avoid accidental political embarrassment or animosity. Just as a good carpenter always measures twice and cuts once, an educator hoping to avoid stepping on a political land mine should read and re-read political articles, essays, and other public information on pertinent political positions on education topics. Stay aware of political ambitions and maneuvers for political office.

- Remember that many school districts have educational and political leaders who have served over an extended period of time. A long tenure guarantees a long memory. Under no circumstance should your actions ever leave a bitter taste for you, your administrator, or your school by school board or community leaders.

At Every Opportunity, Do All You Can to Maintain a Strong Reputation for Your District. Never discredit your district. Discrediting your system by airing dirty laundry publicly will never be viewed as being noble and will undoubtedly seal an impression that you lack loyalty and good sense. Work along established avenues of positive public exposure. Emphasize what is right when trying to repair what is wrong. When power figures realize that you are a trustworthy team member willing to work with honor, they will be far more willing to hear your ideas or suggestions for improvement.

Emphasize what is right when trying to repair what is wrong.

Build Relationships With Other Districts. Only fools insist on re-inventing the wheel. As soon as you feel confident that you have sufficiently studied and followed your own school district's regulations and procedures, you can begin to move beyond its boundaries. Exploring how others approach your job duties and mission goals can be enlightening and rejuvenating. Feel free to join formal and informal associations that can further your areas of interest. As you participate with these various associations, stay alert to shifts in leadership. If a vacancy arises in which you feel you can play a beneficial role, by all means, step up to the plate. Leading an organization that supports special education will expose you to countless other professionals with similar beliefs. These relationships can often bloom into long lasting contacts that encourage significant positive changes in educational reform. Again, keep your administrator in the loop. Often, your administrator will have contacts to offer you as well.

Get the Good Stuff at Local, State, and National Levels. Just as you may pursue being a teacher leader within select organizations, you can also set your sights on becoming a valuable spokesperson for special education at local, state, and national conferences and seminars. Seek endorsement from your administrator to present seminars and workshops that help shape the destiny of American education. Work diligently to present all materials in the most professional manner available. Most large associations and organizations maintain clearinghouses of valuable information and network resources and can also offer other colleagues to contact. Eagerly offer compliments and credit to your supportive administrator for his or her guidance, enthusiasm, and confidence in your endeavors. In fact, many administrators are willing to come to a conference or seminar with you to add their perspective as a school building leader. By getting out there and meeting new people, not only do you invariably fill your car trunk with new classroom goodies to enliven your lesson plans, you also fill your mind with new ideas that will broaden your perspective and expand your philosophy of teaching.

Be Your Own Public Relations Advocate. If you really want to thrive and to make your career a life-long adventure, it is important from the onset to commit to the long haul. Thus, we have Pointer Nine.

POINTER NINE : REMEMBER THAT MOVING THE MOUNTAIN ONE SPOONFUL AT A TIME IS STILL MOVING THE MOUNTAIN

Imagine your career as a hanging mobile. The various items strung for display have all been chosen for their beauty and importance.

Temporary disappointments and setbacks are all a part of the adventure. They can disorient those who lose sight of the mission of their work. It takes courage and fortitude to be a master special educator. Set your anchor with colleagues of integrity and passion. They will teach you, support you, uplift you, and affirm your love of children. Imagine your career as a hanging mobile. The various items strung for display have all been chosen for their beauty and importance. In order to achieve symmetry and balance, the hanging pieces have to be moved and adjusted from time to time as the passing wind flows. The various aspects of your profession also need constant attention and modification as the flow of time changes areas of emphasis and concentration. Have fun in your work, abide by the rules, and squeeze out *every* ounce of your potential before the adventure ends.

POINTER TEN: IT IS <u>ALWAYS</u> ABOUT THE STUDENTS!

As teachers we must remember the power and influence we exert on the young people who depend on us to constantly hone our skills in order to deliver not just good instruction, but outstanding instruction. These students need extraordinary teaching performance. We cannot simply maintain students in classrooms when skills, levels of commitment, and professionalism are not giving them what they require and deserve.

School administrators want you to be the very best. They want no weak links on the chain, and they are dedicated to strengthening the productivity of every staff member. The field of education is not about keeping people employed, and it is not okay to obtain a few years under your belt, achieve tenure, and then glide through the next 27 years with mediocre effort and energy. We have numerous resources all around us if we take the time to look for them. I hope you will make a conscious choice to join the ranks of master teachers who put children first and champion their current and future well-being. The pointers in this chapter have been offered to protect you and the children you serve from the dragons of naiveté, slovenliness, arrogance, negativity, disrespect, self-pity, apathy, ignorance, isolation, and disheartenment. Sail clear of where these dragons live, and enjoy the breeze at your back.

May your hearts be strong and brave throughout your wondrous journey!

Make a conscious choice to join the ranks of master teachers who put children first and champion their current and future well-being.

Collaborating With Professionals and Parents Without Being Overwhelmed: Building Partnerships and Teams

MARILYN FRIEND
UNIVERSITY OF NORTH CAROLINA–GREENSBORO

LYNNE COOK
CALIFORNIA STATE UNIVERSITY, NORTHRIDGE

A former student recently called to ask for help. She was in the middle of one of those complicated situations: A first-grade teacher had a student with autism in her class. The student was on another special educator's caseload, but the classroom teacher asked for Maria's assistance because Maria had extensive experience with students who have autism, and the other special educator did not.

The other special educator was concerned about Maria overstepping her role and had mentioned it to the assistant principal, who then got involved ... and on and on. Maria *explained that she was just trying to be helpful to the first grade teacher and then commented with a sigh, "I'm really confident in my skills for working with the students, and I know I'm making a difference. **But dealing with the <u>adults</u>...that's the real challenge!"***

Understand the tremendous positive potential of collaboration and embrace it as an integral part of being a special educator.

Have you had a similar experience? Perhaps your experience was a difficult interaction with a parent who was upset over something beyond your control. Perhaps you disagreed with a general education teacher's instructional approach, yet you were assigned to co-teach with that individual for the entire school year. Or perhaps you made an unfortunate comment at a team meeting, and you still wonder if your colleagues think a little less of you as a professional. The challenges of working with other teachers, related services providers, paraeducators, administrators, parents, and other adults in school settings can be thought of in two ways: either as a secondary and often difficult responsibility that takes time away from your highest priority — *teaching* — or as an opportunity to engage in partnerships with others to reach students even more effectively than you could alone. We hope that you have come to understand the tremendous positive potential of collaboration and that you embrace it as an integral part of being a special educator.

Collaboration in Context

Before discussing how to make collaboration most successful and what to do when dilemmas occur, it is important to recognize that collaboration is not at all unique to special education or even to education (Friend & Cook, 2003). In fact, educators are relative newcomers to a concept that has become a hallmark of other professions. For example, business professionals learn in their training programs that working together results in greater profits; this notion is implemented when marketers, manufacturers, sales representatives, engineers, and others form teams to create new products. Bennis and Biederman (1997) suggest that the most influential inventions of the last century were only possible because of collaboration. From social services to public health to medicine, collaboration is viewed as a necessity, not a luxury. It is seen as the best vehicle for accomplishing many of the goals that characterize today's complex society.

Current trends in education and special education also will keep collaboration in the forefront for special education teachers. For example, the No Child Left Behind Act of 2001 includes a provision that all students — including those with disabilities — participate in statewide assessments (Council for Exceptional Children, 2002). This increases pressure on special educators to collaborate because their students must have access to the same curriculum as other students. In addition, collaboration continues to be central to middle school philosophy (Park, 1999), school-university partnerships (Johnston, Brosnan, Cramer, & Dove, 2000), and administrative initiatives

Figure 1: IDEA and Collaboration

Collaboration has become an essential special educator skill. IDEA sets a high standard for collaboration between and among professionals, parents, and other service providers (CEC, 2002). Increased expectations are being placed on paraeducators, requiring additional skills of the special education teachers who prepare and supervise them.

Here are some examples of collaboration in action in the federal special education law and regulations:

- At least one general education teacher must participate in the IEP meeting if the student has any part of his or her education in that setting. This brings general and special educators to a shared conversation about students with disabilities.

- A justification must be provided for any student whose least restrictive environment is judged to be a setting other than general education. This fosters shared deliberation.

- Parent participation in all parts of the assessment, eligibility, and programming process is premised on clear and supportive communication. More than ever before, parent collaboration is an expectation.

- The augmented standard for transition planning increases the likelihood that special educators will work with professionals from agencies outside the school.

- The provision that teams complete functional behavior assessments and create behavior intervention plans for students needing such supports creates additional opportunities for interactions among teachers, administrators, counselors, psychologists, and other professionals.

- As attention to the appropriate preparation and supervision for paraeducators increases, additional skills are required of the special education teachers who guide their day-to-day work.

(Wesson & Kudlacz, 2000), as well as many other formal and informal school projects and programs.

The field of special education itself places special emphasis on collaboration. Even before federal laws guaranteed students' rights, special educators were collaborating with each other and professionals in other agencies to achieve success with students. Now most special educators engage in informal collaboration as they work to meet students' educational needs. Further, the Individuals with Disabilities Education Act (IDEA) sets a high expectation for collaboration and undoubtedly will continue to do so, even in future reauthorizations. Figure 1 provides several examples of the many ways special educators, general education teachers, parents, and others are expected to join forces to educate students with disabilities.

Can you see then that collaboration for special educators is being propelled by trends in contemporary society, by initiatives in education, and by regulations emerging from legislation? The importance of collaboration is likely to grow, making it imperative for you to continue to refine your collaboration skills — even when a situation or interaction is awkward or difficult.

Surviving and Thriving Through Collaboration

As is true with so many ideas, talking and writing about collaboration is usually easier than implementing it. Nearly everyone supports the concept of collaboration, and most professionals welcome collaboration when it involves friends or colleagues with whom they are comfortable and when the matter at hand is relatively innocuous. When collaboration can matter most, though, is when the participants do not have a close relationship or when the interaction involves controversy. Here are some ideas for making your collaboration as constructive as possible.

To Collaborate or Not ~ That Is the Question

Collaboration should be reserved for instances in which multiple perspectives are valuable and for which adequate time can be created.

One of the first questions about working with others is whether it is worth the time and effort that will be involved. Collaboration is expensive in two ways: First, there is a personnel cost in collaboration. Given the number of students with special needs and the limited number of professionals to meet those needs, careful attention must be paid to whether two, three, or more people's efforts are best used working together to address a problem, or whether that matter could be as effectively addressed by just one person. Second, the length of time it takes to collaborate is a significant consideration. When professionals share decision making, they need to allocate enough time for interactions that provide each participant with a voice in the discussion. Decisions made alone are much more time-efficient. These two points suggest that collaboration should be reserved for instances in which multiple perspectives are particularly valuable and for which adequate time can be created.

What does all this mean in practice? Here are a few questions that you might ask to help yourself decide whether collaboration is a good choice.

QUESTION ONE: *To what extent does the problem, project, or program affect more than just me? Could this problem, project, or program be addressed with clear and positive communication from me without collaboration?*

In some cases, the purpose in initiating collaboration may be to interest others in a particular matter; in other cases this is not a valid reason to seek collaboration. For example, even though you may wish to interest a general education teacher in learning to adapt the social studies textbook, it may be more realistic to complete the highlighting and supplemental study guide yourself because both of you are very busy. However, if the task at hand is deciding how to arrange instruction during the co-taught social studies class, both teachers are directly affected; the effort to collaborate definitely has an impact on the result. Perhaps you have interacted with a mother who is over-whelmed and does not have time to come to school for a discussion of her child's behavior. Be realistic; even if you sincerely wish to form a partnership with the parent, it might be best to create a positive support system at school and to communicate with the parent via telephone, notes home, or e-mail about that support system. If you were to insist on substantial parent involve-ment, you might be disappointed and incorrectly assume the parent does not care.

QUESTION TWO: *How necessary is it for others to make a strong com-mitment to participating?*

The parent example in question one demonstrates that sometimes commit-ment can exist even though participation is not possible. This question, how-ever, considers the opposite: whether you should seek collaboration when others are not committed to it. For example, sometimes in a team meeting a multi-faceted intervention is discussed, and several members strongly favor implementing it. However, one member — perhaps the teacher who works most closely with the student — expresses reluctance to engage in designing the contract, working with the playground supervisor, and inviting the social worker to the classroom. Before this extensive collaboration is pursued, it is critical that everyone, especially the teacher, strongly agrees to it.

> **Before this extensive collaboration is pursued, it is critical that everyone, especially the teacher, strongly agrees to it.**

QUESTION THREE: *To what extent are mechanisms in place to foster collaboration?*

In some schools, special educators would like to expand their collaborative efforts; but they are constrained by the school schedule, the ways in which teacher lunches and preparation periods are created, and the number of duties teachers have. For example, teams can be extraordinarily successful in designing creative solutions to challenging student behavior — but only if they meet on a regular basis with all members in attendance. Consultation can effectively address some students' instructional needs, but only if the con-sultant and the teacher can meet to engage in the consulting process.

QUESTION FOUR: *What are the intended outcomes of the collaboration? How will we know if we have accomplished our goal?*

Collaboration is a vehicle for reaching a goal; it is not a goal in itself. Therefore, it is important for you and other participants to work together to specify outcomes that will signal that the collaboration is concluded and that it has been a success. Learning from parents' perspectives, enjoying the camaraderie that develops through effective collaboration, and benefiting from the growing trust and respect collaborators experience have merit only if the collaboration results in positive outcomes for students.

Laying the Groundwork ~
Establishing and Building Relationships

The decisions you make about whether the activity at hand is appropriate for collaboration lead you to collaboration itself. Collaboration emerges; it sometimes begins with a rather cautious or formal feeling until participants learn more about each other and recognize that their trust is well-placed and that their respect for each other is warranted. Eventually a sense of community develops. Further, when a collaborative partnership is relatively new, it is fragile; even unintended miscommunication can damage the relationships. To reach the point of strength and community, a strong foundation should be built.

A basic ingredient in collaboration is direct and clear communication with other participants.

A basic ingredient in collaboration is direct and clear communication with other participants. This means, first, that all participants directly address the purpose and expectations of their shared work. Is the team meeting to design additional interventions for a student or to determine whether a referral to special education is appropriate? Is the goal of the meeting with the parent to learn the parent's perspective on the challenge being encountered or to explain to the parent what actions the school professionals would like to take? Second, communication pertains to roles and responsibilities. In co-teaching, for example, have you discussed with your teaching partner what you would consider an ideal arrangement? Have you listened to your partner's perception and then negotiated with him or her so that both of you are satisfied with in-class roles and responsibilities?

A third area in which clear communication is needed is monitoring. When does your team take a few minutes to discuss how effectively it is functioning and whether any members would like to raise concerns? When do you and your co-teaching partner discuss how well your arrangement is meeting student needs and whether you might try some additional ways to engage the students? Finally, and perhaps most importantly, groundwork includes keeping your administrator informed. Have you and other collaborators met with him or her to discuss your plans and progress?

Schools are hectic places, and you may sometimes feel like you barely have the time to complete the most basic parts of your job, much less reflect on your work and discuss with colleagues how you form partnerships. School structures sometimes inadvertently contribute to this sense: Have you experienced the anxiety created when you are informed the day before school begins that you are supposed to co-teach with a general education teacher? And then, when you sought that teacher out and explained that you were the assigned co-teacher, the teacher offered a puzzled expression and said, "We're doing what? Teaching together? When was this decided?" We wish this didn't occur; but it does, sometimes for understandable reasons such as staffing changes. Your responsibility in such situations, though, is to slow down enough to establish a strong basis for your year's work with that individual. Simply rushing into the collaboration and agreeing to whatever role the teacher assumes you should have can be a recipe for frustration for you and the students.

Encountering Bumps in the Road

An entire book could be written about the complexities of working with other adults in school settings. Bumps in the road when you are collaborating with others should not be viewed as extraordinary. They should instead be considered inevitable, because the power of collaboration resides largely in the marriage of differing perspectives. But those differing perspectives also create misunderstandings and disagreements. When bumps occur, thinking and acting constructively strengthens the collaboration and re-affirms your professional skills.

Collaboration is characterized by subtlety, and seldom does just one factor contribute to a problem in the relationship. Perhaps participants have differing views on the value of reading instruction in middle school. This difference of opinion is magnified when one person has a negative experience with a general education teacher over a reading assignment. Perhaps discussion of this episode was overheard by yet another participant who then reported it to another. Without any additional detail, you probably know exactly how such things happen. Eventually, tension develops or disagreements surface, and the well-intended collaborative efforts slow or even halt. Since you can't avoid occasional trouble spots in collaboration, the best way to address them — even if it's not easy — is to recognize the signals early and resolve the matter before it grows. If you learn to attend closely to the ways your colleagues indicate discomfort or disagreement and also learn your own signals, you can spend less time worrying about such issues and more time engaged in constructive collaboration. Figure 2 provides some examples of signals that might indicate it is time for a collaboration tune-up.

The best way to address trouble spots — even if it's not easy — is to recognize the signals early and resolve the matter before it grows.

Collaboration is all about communication — verbal and nonverbal — and issues are laid to rest by airing them, getting agreement, and moving on. The longer you wait to raise an issue that you know is becoming a point of contention, the more difficult it is to do so with confidence, directness, and a positive outlook. Hoping that a controversial matter will take care of itself, discussing with a colleague in another school district your difference of opinion with your co-teacher, overlooking a colleague's silence, or using silence yourself to express disagreement — these strategies provide brief and false comfort. Figure 3 provides an outline of the steps to take if you encounter collaboration bumps, and here are a few suggestions to supplement them:

Practice Exemplary Communication Skills. If you wish to raise a problem with others, keep ownership of it. That is, use language such as, "I'm concerned about Rashid's behavior plan. I'm not convinced it's effective," instead of saying, "Don't you think we should consider other options for Rashid's behavior plan?" The former is an expression of an opinion; the latter is veiled pressure for someone else to agree with your point of view.

Aim for Understanding First, Resolving Later. When someone else, perhaps a parent, makes a comment to you such as, "I just don't think my child is getting the best education possible this year," a common intuitive reaction

Figure 2: Potential Bumps in the Collaboration Road

Even skilled and experienced collaborators encounter difficulties in their work with other adults in school. When you see these signals, it may be time to proceed with caution, seek assistance from others, or reflect carefully on communication patterns. A bump may be looming when

~ any person involved in the collaboration seems to be speaking less and providing less information to conversations. (**Example:** Leigh rolls her eyes when Karen offers an idea. Karen asks if Leigh has concerns about the intervention, but Leigh says, "No. It's fine." This type of exchange happens several times.)

~ any person involved in the collaboration seems to be avoiding certain topics or discussing those topics with others outside the collaborative work context. (**Example:** One team member seems always to come to meetings late and sometimes leaves early, even though everyone had agreed to the meeting time. Or certain team members discuss the issue outside the team meeting, and everyone is aware that it is a problem, but members do not broach the topic when everyone is present.)

~ any person involved in the collaboration is failing to follow through on commitments, a detriment to reaching the shared goal. (**Example:** The general education teacher keeps "forgetting" that the special educator needs a copy of next week's lesson plans in order to plan accommodations for students with disabilities in the class. Variations on this example are when a general education teacher does not provide a copy of a test needing adaptations to the special educator until the morning it is to be given, and when a special educator promises to load, learn, and teach a new piece of software to several students in a class, but never seems to quite have the time to carry out the commitment.)

~ any participant in the collaboration senses tension and/or conflict. (**Example:** At a team meeting, one member suddenly walks out of the room, closing the door with what some might call a slam. In an interaction between a special educator and parent, eye contact suddenly becomes difficult and either person's body language conveys withdrawal from the interaction.)

is to become defensive or to ask the parent what the problem is. An alternative is to again respond with an "I" statement: "I'm not sure what you mean...(silence)." By gently asking the parent to share additional information you may find out that the parent is simply noticing greater gaps in the child's learning this year, may be missing a favorite teacher from last year, or may have misinformation. Your response will be more effective if you first understand the concern.

Avoid Language That May Push Buttons for Others. If a teacher is concerned about working with a student with special needs, repeatedly referring

Figure 3: Steps for Addressing Bumps in the Collaboration Road

When an awkward, difficult, or resistant interaction occurs during collaboration, these are the steps you should take with all the other participants to ensure that everything gets back on track. The more serious the controversy and the longer it has existed, the more essential it is to address each step directly:

- Reconfirm the purpose of the collaborative effort.

- Re-assess each participant's commitment to the collaboration.

- Re-examine each participant's roles and responsibilities, clarifying as necessary.

- Identify and discuss what appears to be the source of the difficulty, making sure that these conversations focus on resolution rather than blame.

- Decide on specific action steps to alleviate the difficulty. These should be written down and individual responsibility assigned as appropriate.

- Identify clear criteria for deciding whether the steps being taken are helping to resolve the dilemma.

- Set a specific time for a meeting to discuss the status on the difficulty.

If you follow these steps, even the most contentious issues and awkward situations can be dealt with in a constructive and professional manner; and you probably will find that when the matter is resolved, you'll feel positive about the outcome and even more committed to collaboration than you were before.

to inclusion may not be wise. Some parents may react to terms that special educators do not find objectionable, even the term disability.

After all the attempts to communicate, you may find that collaboration is not possible or has deteriorated to the point that some action must be taken. You may have used effective communication skills and tried to problem solve constructively, and you are working diligently to be positive and direct. But it still seems that what you thought was a bump feels more and more like a wall. It is critical that you learn to recognize this point. Although difficult to face, this is another reality of collaboration. It may occur in co-teaching when a general education teacher insists that you sit quietly until delivery of large group instruction has ended and then help the students needing your assistance. Despite several conversations about your discomfort with and the inappropriateness of this role, the teacher is adamant that you only have this limited classroom responsibility. On a team, perhaps conflict has mounted quietly to the point that several members have spoken harsh words to one another. The atmosphere of the meeting is now tension-charged. It might also happen that a parent demands a particular program

You may use effective communication skills and try to be positive and direct, but it still seems that what you thought was a bump feels more like a wall.

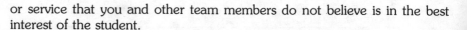

or service that you and other team members do not believe is in the best interest of the student.

In these and many other situations, we hope that you will accept the fact that it is not solely your responsibility to fix what is amiss. Often, this is the time to involve a special education coordinator, district consultant, principal, or another qualified but more removed party who may be able to facilitate a more productive outcome. In some cases, particularly if a principal or another administrator clarifies expectations, collaboration can proceed. But it may take time to mend broken avenues of communication, and the partnership may never have the sense of closeness that exists in your other collaborative work. In some matters regarding parents, you need to recognize that a legal issue may be at stake and seek the assistance that can lead to resolution instead of mediation. Once in awhile, if the setting in which you work is not supportive of collaboration, and you repeatedly encounter extreme difficulty, you may decide that you would be happier in another school. That is a drastic move and not to be taken lightly, but it should not be completely ruled out.

Conclusion

Although collaboration can be an incredibly useful way to go about the business of being a special education teacher, it is not the only approach; nor is it always the best approach. Because collaboration is a tremendously complex endeavor, often there is no single correct answer to questions about nurturing collaboration and addressing the challenges that invariably come with it. The need to collaborate with specific individuals and the outcomes you can expect from collaboration change from year to year as the characteristics and needs of your students and their families change. Time will also reveal a varying willingness to collaborate on the part of other special educators, related services personnel, the principal, and general education teachers in your school. It also can depend on the school's environment (such as adequate space and time) and the overall context for creating partnerships among staff and with parents.

Collaboration is an area for life-long professional development, a potential source of power and satisfaction.

Collaboration is an area for life-long professional development, never to be completely mastered but always a potential source of power and satisfaction. The power is the legitimate and best kind — it is when others value what you have to offer and listen carefully to your ideas because they respect you, trust you, and find that you are a colleague who keeps the ultimate goal of students' education always in mind. The satisfaction derives from building strong and effective professional relationships with your co-workers and with parents, and being aware that these relationships magnify the impact you have on the lives of students with disabilities.

References

Bennis, W., & Biederman, P. W. (1997). *Organizing genius: The secrets of creative collaboration*. Reading, MA: Addison-Wesley.

Council for Exceptional Children. (2002). No Child Left Behind Act of 2001: Reauthorization of the Elementary and Secondary Education Act: A technical assistance resource. Retrieved November 2, 2002, from http://www.cec.sped.org/pp/OverviewNCLB.pdf

Friend, M., & Cook, L. (2003). *Interactions: Collaboration skills for school professionals* (4th edition, pp. 1–25). Boston: Allyn & Bacon.

Johnston, M., Brosnan, P., Cramer, D., & Dove, T. (Eds.). (2000). *Collaborative reform and other improbable dreams*. Albany, NY: State University of New York Press.

Park, E. (1999). Making a team effort [Electronic version]. Collaboration is an area for life-long professional development. *Schools in the Middle, 8*(7), 35-38.

Wesson, L., & Kudlacz, J. M. (2000). Collaboration for change [Electronic version]. *Principal Leadership, 1*(3), 50-53.

Chapter
4

Maximizing the Services
of Paraeducators

NANCY K. FRENCH
DIRECTOR, THE PAR^{2}A CENTER
UNIVERSITY OF COLORADO AT DENVER

As you crossed the threshold of your first classroom, you may have been greeted by a paraeducator who has had experience assisting other special educators. Or you may be paired with a paraeducator who is as new as you are to the job. Both of these scenarios are fraught with potential difficulties. In this chapter, we consider an important theme: making the shift from thinking like a novice and beginning to think like a leader. When you have made this shift, you will be able to avoid many difficulties and to maximize the services of your assistants.

Paraeducators (also known as educational assistants, teacher aides, paraprofessionals, or instructional assistants) work alongside professional educators. This does not necessarily mean, however, that the paraeducator always works in your line of vision. Think of a busy orthodontist's office. While the orthodontist is working with one patient, it is likely that the dental technician is removing the wires from the appliances of another, as directed by the

The special education teacher must clearly delineate between teacher and paraeducator roles.

orthodontist. Later, when the orthodontist examines the patient, the technician goes to work with someone else. The orthodontist notes the work of the technician and assesses the progress of the patient. Based on the progress, the orthodontist determines the next step in the treatment plan, decides on any necessary changes in the appliances, shapes new wires or devices, and gives directions to the technician. Just as the orthodontist determines and directs the treatment plan, uses the skills of the dental technician wisely, and delineates between the role of the technician and that of the orthodontist, so must the special education teacher plan and direct the individualized programs of his or her students, use the skills of the paraeducator wisely, and clearly delineate between teacher and paraeducator roles.

Unfortunately, guidance for directing the work of paraeducators is typically provided perfunctorily, if at all, during teacher preparation programs. You may well find yourself not knowing what to do when faced with the reality of directing an assistant in a real classroom. The following eight pointers may help you become more self-assured about working with paraeducators.

POINTER ONE: ESTABLISH GOOD WORKING RELATIONSHIPS WITH OTHER PROFESSIONALS

In the previous chapter, you found information about establishing and building working relationships with other professionals who also serve your students. Those working relationships are essential to your ability to maximize the effectiveness of the paraeducators you supervise. The paraeducator cannot replace you in professional relationships or in your interactions with families and parents. A paraeducator should not be asked to intercede between professionals or between you and parents, nor should a paraeducator "consult" with classroom teachers or parents. If a classroom teacher serves special education students, it is the responsibility of the special educator to develop a working relationship with that teacher and provide directions to the paraeducator based on the shared goals and responsibility for the child. Likewise, it is clearly the role of the teacher to communicate with parents.

POINTER TWO: ACT LIKE A LEADER

Acting like a leader is a tall order for a novice teacher. But as you continue in the profession and grow with it, you will gradually be able to assume the qualities of a leader while learning leadership functions. As your leadership skills develop, you will become more and more like a mid-level executive or manager who holds certain responsibilities for leading a business. As a professional educator, you will plan, direct, train, coach, schedule, and monitor the work of the paraeducator. And you must do all this while taking responsibility for assessing and planning for your students. While the paraeducator is a potential asset in ensuring that your students get the instruction they deserve — in freeing up your time to do other things — your leadership is the factor that will either limit or enhance the development of a paraeducator's potential.

POINTER THREE: CLARIFY YOUR ROLES

To exercise your leadership, you need to clearly understand the difference in roles of professional educator and paraeducator. As team leader, you will want to clarify this distinction to the paraeducators with whom you work. Table 1, next page, demonstrates how the roles of the professional and paraeducator are similar and different in each domain.

POINTER FOUR: CLARIFY SPECIFIC JOB DUTIES

Letting the paraeducator know what you expect of him or her is another leadership skill. However, deciding what you need paraeducators to do in your program, within ethical and legal standards, program type, student ages and needs, is not an easy task. First year teachers are rarely able to think ahead or anticipate all that will need to be done. But with a year or two under your belt, you can now begin to anticipate the kinds of assistance you'll need and the kinds of activities that you expect paraeducators to do with students. Expect to spend some time clarifying job duties: Once you make these clear, however, you will have a basis for your work with paraeducators. The right-hand column of Table 1 suggests categories of tasks that need to be done. None of these tasks should go beyond the scope of the official district job description, but you should describe them in more detail. This detailed list of tasks clarifies your expectations to the paraeducator.

POINTER FIVE: MAKE THE BEST USE OF THE PARAEDUCATOR'S TIME AND SKILL

How do you know what skills the paraeducator has? Well, in your first year or two of teaching, you probably found out gradually by observing what the paraeducator did. However, a shorter and more accurate route to discovering a paraeducator's skills is the use of a "self-report." You can quickly and easily assess what a paraeducator knows, where the paraeducator's talents lie, and where specific skills can be best employed in your program. Simply use the master list of tasks you created, and ask the paraeducator to indicate to you the level of confidence or the amount of experience he or she has with each task. This self-report has been shown to be the single best indicator of what the paraeducator is capable of doing. The self-report also tells you which tasks you will have to train your paraeducators to do.

The self-report has been shown to be the single best indicator of what the paraeducator is capable of doing.

POINTER SIX: PROVIDE ORIENTATION

By now you may be noticing that leadership skills are not esoteric or mysterious. Leadership functions are really quite basic. The next leadership function is providing orientation to new employees or to paraeducators that you are just starting to work with. Orientation is based on good common sense. Just as you would introduce guests in your home, take time to introduce your paraeducators to one another and to teachers and employees in the building. You will want to show new people where to keep their personal belong-

Table 1: Roles of Professionals vs. Paraeducators

Domain	Professional Educator Role	Paraeducator Role
General safety procedures and policies	Make sure written and non-written procedures and policies that guide student safety and welfare are given to paraeducators.	Fully understand and abide by written safety procedures.
Classroom rules and staff introductions	Orient paraeducators to classroom/program rules, routines, procedures, and practices and introduce them to their co-workers.	Carry out and support all classroom/program rules, routines, procedures, and practices.
Student risks and limitations	Decide appropriate risks as well as limitations for students. Communicate this information to paraeducators.	Exercise prudent judgment relative to the safety and welfare of students.
Instructional plans and adaptations	Assess and plan for your students. Create written plans that guide instruction and adaptations and provide them to paraeducators.	Implement the written instructional, curricular, and adaptation plans as directed.
Record keeping	Establish and maintain a record keeping system so paraeducators contribute data about student behavior and progress that help you as you make student plans and account to parents.	Take data, keep appropriate records and documentation relative to student performance and behavior, and contribute to the record keeping system.
Schedule expectations	Create a master schedule for yourself and paraeducators.	Follow the schedule, be on time, carry out duties as listed on the schedule.
Communication, coordination	Communicate your decisions and plans to paraeducators and coordinate your work, as needed, with other professionals.	Communicate all relevant observations, insights, or information about students to professional educators.
Individual student safety and welfare needs	Review with paraeducators all of the needs or circumstances of students that may affect their safety or welfare (e.g., health issues, behavior patterns).	Be aware of and heed the physical, behavioral, emotional, and educational needs of students that may affect their safety and welfare.

ings during the day, where to put their lunches, where to eat lunch, and where the adult rest rooms are.

Orientation also means that you provide the paraeducator with all the same written information that a teacher would receive in your building. If your school has a staff handbook containing school procedures, rules, policies, and so forth, make sure each paraeducator has a copy and that you've reviewed the contents together. Orientation is also the time to go over the list of tasks you've created and to ask the paraeducator to reflect on his or her own skills and confidence levels on those tasks. If you do this step, paraeducators will begin to see you as a leader and, more importantly, they will know what you expect of them.

Orientation is the time to go over the list of tasks and ask the paraeducator to reflect on his or her skills.

POINTER SEVEN: PLAN AND MONITOR THE PARAEDUCATOR'S WORK WITH STUDENTS

During the first few years of teaching it is difficult to anticipate what needs to be done next; therefore, many novice teachers have tremendous difficulty delegating tasks to others. As you begin to see yourself effectively delegating tasks to paraeducators, you will know that you have achieved that transition point to becoming a career professional. Several tips may help you ensure that your delegation does not inadvertently become *"dumping," "passing the buck," "puppeteering,"* or *"punishment."*

Avoid Dumping. Make sure that paraeducators know what to do and how to do it. You may have to take the time to teach them how you want tasks done, why you want them to work with a child in a certain way, why challenging behaviors are handled in certain ways, and so on.

Beware of Passing the Buck. Remember that ultimate responsibility for student progress toward IEP goals is yours. Paraeducators should be part of the system for reaching those goals, but you are the one that is accountable in the end. Be sure to think carefully about what needs to be done to reach student goals and objectives, and be planful or judicious about the tasks you assign to the paraeducator. Judicious delegation means that you have considered the ethics and liability associated with assigning a task to someone else rather than doing it yourself.

Provide Work Plans to Avoid Puppeteering. Provide each paraeducator with work plans that contain vital information from the IEP, such as student strengths and needs, agreed-upon adaptations (including the circumstances under which each adaptation is deemed appropriate), purposes of various types of activities and lessons, and information on steps, materials, and timeframes.

Ensure That Students' Goals Are Being Addressed and That Students Are Making Adequate Progress Toward Goals. Include a feedback system so that paraeducators report back to you every day in writing about student performance. Request hard data. For example, if a paraeducator is working with a student on the use of an assistive communication device, ask the paraeducator to record the number of spontaneous uses of the device and require that the level of prompting be quantified for every use. Or if the paraeducator is working with a group of students on vocabulary drill and practice, ask the paraeducator to provide the number of correct and incorrect responses each student made during the time he or she worked with the group. These data allow you to maintain your accountability even when you are not physically present to watch the paraeducator work with students.

Finally, Avoid Making Tasks Seem Punishing. If you are assisted by two or more paraeducators, distribute assignments fairly among them and occasionally pitch in on the tasks that are less pleasant. You can also reduce the punishing aspects of tasks if you take care to find out what a person prefers doing and provide adequate opportunity to do those things as well as the things that are less preferred. Changing diapers is a task that tends to be less preferred, for example. Rotating and sharing this task is important for team morale and fairness.

Remember there are many good reasons to delegate, plan, and monitor the work of paraeducators. Delegation maximizes your own time by emphasizing getting the job done while de-emphasizing doing it yourself. Good delegation, based on ethical assignment of tasks, means that you are getting more "bang for your buck" — more done with students than you could possibly do yourself. It also means that your students win!

POINTER EIGHT: ESTABLISH AND USE EFFECTIVE COMMUNICATION

Providing feedback to paraeducators about their work is a crucially important element of communication. It allows paraeducators to know you have heard their input and observed their work. Take time to let paraeducators know which of the assigned tasks you see them doing well and which ones they need to work on.

The opposite of assertive leadership is passivity, which is certain to sabotage your leadership efforts.

Make a note to yourself to provide additional training and assistance on tasks they don't do well. A positive, assertive approach assumes that they need additional training on tasks they don't do well. The opposite of assertive leadership is passivity, which is certain to sabotage your leadership efforts. Avoid taking a passive-aggressive approach in which you simply stop assigning appropriate tasks because a paraeducator fails to perform the task on time, fails to perform it correctly, or complains about it. *You are the leader:* If you encounter paraeducator behavior that is not helpful, use positive, assertive communications, and provide support in the areas where it is most needed.

In fact, the most important aspect of building a good working relationship with the paraeducator in your program is to remind yourself to always use assertive communication techniques. Too often, passive-aggressive or passive-resistant behaviors ruin a team that could be effective if other communication styles were used. Set team meetings. Schedule time during the workday — your best work with students will result if you take the time to meet with the paraeducator during the day. Use the meeting time to speak honestly about tasks that need to be done, to guide paraeducator performance of those tasks, and to train the paraeducator to perform new tasks. You can also use a regularly scheduled meeting time to solve problems and resolve conflicts. Remember, conflicts are inevitable. Good people who work together will have conflicts — conflicts that arise from different perspectives. Take time to resolve conflicts, and you will be free to be the best teacher-paraeducator team possible!

Take time to resolve conflicts, and you will be free to be the best teacher-paraeducator team possible!

Reference

French, N. K. (2003). *Managing paraeducators in your school: How to hire, train, and supervise non-certified staff*. Thousand Oaks, CA: Corwin Press.

**Chapter
5**

Making Paperwork Work
for You and Your Students

Lynne Cook
K. Sarah Hall
California State University, Northridge

Like most special educators, you undoubtedly entered the profession to teach students with disabilities and to make a difference in their lives. By now, you've probably discovered the conflicting demands of completing paperwork and using your time effectively for teaching students. While we cannot eliminate paperwork or the need for it, we can suggest strategies for handling it more effectively and efficiently without reducing its value. In this chapter we sort through some of the paperwork issues, take a new look at related tasks, and outline strategies for limiting the extent to which paperwork interrupts effective teaching.

As special education professionals, we were taught to rely on systematic observation, assessment, and related data collection to determine student needs and to assess student progress and program success. Many methods that have proven effective for students with unique learning needs require record keeping and paperwork. Moreover, as professionals in special education, we are committed to the Council for Exceptional Children's Code of Ethics and Standards for Professional Practice for Special Education (CEC, 2003), which requires us to uphold and comply with the laws and regulations governing the delivery of services, provide accurate program data based on efficient and objective record keeping practices, and base decisions upon documented performance relative to students' Individualized Education Plans (IEPs). Some of these professional commitments are outlined in Figure 1.

Figure 1: Some Professional Commitments

Ethical Tenets

Special education professionals seek to uphold and improve where necessary the laws, regulations, and policies governing the delivery of special education and related services and the practice of their profession.

Standards of Practice

Special education professionals

- provide accurate program data to administrators, colleagues, and parents, based on efficient and objective record keeping practices, for the purpose of decision making;

- identify and use instructional methods and curricula that are appropriate to their area of professional practice and effective in meeting the individual needs of persons with exceptionalities; and

- base grading, promotion, graduation, and/or movement out of the program on the individual goals and objectives for individuals with exceptionalities.

Source: CEC (2003).

Sorting Through the Paperwork Issue

So why is "paperwork" now such a bad word? Perhaps because it seems that there is a lot of it, it is often uncoordinated, and it requires greater time and case management skills than we may have learned. Paperwork in special education is associated with developing IEPs, tracking and documenting students' progress, analyzing and providing information to others, and facing additional challenges that are part of being a special educator. Perhaps we are actually using the term paperwork to include these other challenges, and the term may serve as a proxy for these associated activities. If this is the case, we cannot suggest effective strategies for managing paperwork before we look at the contexts and activities that generate paperwork.

Determine the Context of Paperwork. As special educators, we work with students who have highly complex needs that require specialized instructional plans. These plans often require additional services, and we are required to monitor them. In addition, the successive reauthorizations of the Individuals with Disabilities Education Act (IDEA) and the proliferation of other state and federal mandates for data collection and record keeping have added new paperwork requirements that are often assigned to special educators. Think of the number of students for whom you are required to provide written reports or documentation concerning behavior plans, medication schedules, assistive technology needs, and so on. These monitoring requirements are necessary, yet they are being required for the very same students who also need *more* of our teaching time and attention, not less.

List the Activities that Generate Paperwork. Although the paperwork challenge is real and has increased over time, we believe that it is often a proxy that includes other things. What, then, are the real burdens that are represented by paperwork? Our interactions with teachers in hundreds of schools suggest that the true burdens associated with paperwork include (a) collecting data from multiple records and professionals, (b) arranging meeting times, (c) making parent contacts, and (d) exchanging information with other professionals — all activities that require paperwork and may interfere with instructional time.

Although the paperwork challenge is real and has increased over time, we believe that it is often a proxy for associated time-consuming tasks.

The preceding list of tasks sounds simple enough, but we all understand the complexity of the elements involved in each. Many of these tasks involve working with colleagues, parents, and paraeducators. The challenges of working with parents, administrators, peers, and government entities have been addressed in other chapters of this book, so we do not address them here except to recognize that often it is the people problems connected to paperwork that special educators find most daunting.

Time-Saving Guidelines for Special Educators

A number of guidelines for saving time apply to special education, just as they do to any other profession. But because special education poses many challenges, and some of the solutions are unique to our field, we need to examine both general and specific solutions that have proven successful.

STREAMLINE CLASSROOM MANAGEMENT

Because paperwork appears to be a proxy for associated time-consuming tasks, there is also a possibility that paperwork may be a proxy for *all* non-instructional time. Efficient classroom management to maximize instructional time and minimize non-instructional time can make the paperwork burden much lighter. The time teachers spend engaged in instruction is influenced by factors such as standardized testing days, pre-holiday activities, classroom schedules, and related arrangements. But other sources of down time, long settling-in routines, and repeated directions are all non-instructional activities that take time away from teaching (Smith, 2000). In practice, the hours of non-instructional time vary greatly from teacher to teacher. But one fact is clear: Students in less well-managed classrooms receive less formal instruction, and paperwork is not the culprit. Before going about trying to reduce paperwork, it is a good idea to consider whether other management and job-related expectations are detracting from instructional time and may be getting classified as paperwork.

BANISH PAPER CLUTTER

Equally as important as classroom management is learning to manage the basic paper clutter that regularly invades our lives. Some teachers seem to be naturally organized, neat, and tidy, while others have desks and classrooms that always appear to be in chaos. Clutter and chaos seriously reduce opportunities for increased instructional time (see Box 1). Fortunately, organizational skills and strategies for managing paper can be learned. Even when preservice programs include an emphasis on these skills, there may not be adequate time to prepare teacher candidates who have had very little experience with paper management. If you recognize that you need these skills or want to brush up on them, there are numerous texts, online courses, and CD-ROMs on the topic (e.g., http://www.get-ahead.direct.com/gatime.htm).

> **Box 1: Clutter Equals Wasted Time**
>
> - **Keeping your desk clean and free of clutter allows you to focus on the task at hand.**
>
> - **Studies have shown that a person with a messy desk may spend over an hour a day looking for things or being distracted by the clutter.**
>
> - **That's over 5 hours per week that could be used to ease the paperwork burden!**

USE EXISTING RESOURCES FOR TIME MANAGEMENT

Professional time management programs and workshops have long been an accepted practice for business executives — and as educators, our management challenges are just as great as, if not greater than, those that present themselves in business. Such programs have been used successfully by many teachers and are an option to consider. However, the best way for teachers to develop or reinforce their time management skills is through in-services or on-site sharing and mentoring by school staff familiar with the demands of the system and sensitive to system constraints. Box 2 identifies some basic principles as listed in the Web site, http://teacher.scholastic.com/professional/classmgmt/timemanage.htm (Parks, n.d.).

Uncovering Paperwork Demands

Having separated the actual paperwork from related issues, we can talk about the types and purposes of the documents special educators have to handle. There are several approaches to coordinating and making meaning of what often seem to be disjointed tasks and documents. Both formal and informal documentation requirements can be used to communicate with parents, students, and other educators.

KNOW THE ACTUAL REQUIREMENTS OF FORMAL PAPERWORK

> **Box 2: Some Strategies for Saving Time**
>
> • **Identify time robbers.**
>
> • **Learn to say no.**
>
> • **Delegate students to help with routine tasks.**
>
> • **Schedule recoup time into your planning book.**
>
> • **Critically appraise how you spend your time.**
>
> Source: Selected from "Seven Time-Management Sanity Savers" (Parks, n.d.).

Considerable documentation is needed to comply with federal, state, and local policies for educating students with disabilities. The IEP or the Individualized Family Services Plan (IFSP) are two critically important documents that have been expanded significantly in recent years. Sometimes the expanded requirements are duplicative, as is the case with behavior plans that are now included in both IEPs and IFSPs in many states. However, misconceptions about these new requirements can counter the efforts to reduce paperwork. For example, behavioral plans only need to be included if a child's behavior impedes his or her learning or that of other students. And, although transition plans are required for students at a certain age, it may not be necessary to prepare a separate transition document if the services needed by the student can be addressed in the IEP.

Behavioral plans only need to be included if a child's behavior impedes his or her learning or that of other students.

Although more complex in many ways, the IEP survives. It must survive, for it is a contract that guarantees the services a student needs. Often, to protect themselves from litigation, state and local educational agencies require additional documentation beyond that required by federal regulations, resulting in even more paperwork. In discussing the U.S. Department of Education, Office of Special Education Programs' review of paperwork required by states, the National Education Association (NEA) reported, "One IEP package that was sent in was 43 pages long.... [T]he educators were told that most of what they were documenting was unnecessary under the new federal law" (Green, 2000). In fact, the Department of Education's sample IEP form is only five pages long. Table 1 lists a number of common myths about requirements for IEP preparation in contrast to factual requirements.

In many
districts,
teachers are
joining
with local
administrators
to streamline
paperwork and
related
processes.

This excessive reporting on IEP packages is not lost on teacher organizations. CEC has long advocated reducing paperwork and eliminating documentation of short-term objectives. In many districts, teachers are joining with local administrators to streamline paperwork and related processes. Schools are developing creative ways to provide financial support for tracking paperwork, including paying part-time aides and clerical workers for additional hours of support and making arrangements for release time. Some solutions by districts, including hiring substitutes to cover classrooms so teachers can attend IEP meetings, recognize the time constraints on teachers but do not succeed in increasing teacher time in instruction.

Table 1: Myths About the IEP

Myth	Fact
The teacher has to write the IEP.	The team is responsible for the IEP, but the teacher should take leadership in developing instructional objectives.
Students with an IEP are to be retested every 3 years.	Student reevaluation is required every 3 years, but retesting may not be necessary. The IEP team should review existing data before determining if additional data or testing are needed.
Decisions called for in an IEP are difficult for the teacher or team to make.	Professionals and families together have the expertise to make decisions in the best interest of the child.
Completing the IEP document is a significant burden that detracts from the special educators' instructional time.	Preparing for and arranging the IEP meeting are often more time consuming than completing the IEP document.
Teachers can't discuss or do paperwork for an IEP ahead of an IEP meeting.	Teachers can meet to discuss and even write a draft IEP, as long as they do not make final decisions. Teachers can also share a draft with the student's parents, as long as they present it as only an option. Communicating and relating with parents and professionals before the IEP meeting is both effective and is the best practice.
Every IEP needs to contain a behavioral goal.	IEP goals are only written in areas of need. If a student's difficulties are only in reading, it is not necessary to write behavioral goals.

Other formally required documentation includes reports from locally adopted progress monitoring systems, testing and assessment results, reports for related services providers, and other required student performance reports such as behavior reports or medical observations.

MAKE INFORMAL PAPERWORK DO DOUBLE-DUTY

Because grading, promotion, graduation, and/or movement out of the program are based on the goals, benchmarks, and objectives for specific learners with exceptionalities, individualized and often informal records must be kept for students. These typically include informal reports of student progress, student schedules, and anecdotal records. Samples of student work are generally considered informal records. The marking, recording, and maintaining of records related to student work may create additional paperwork. A number of time-saving suggestions are offered by Kronowitz (1992), including:

Informal records typically include reports of student progress, student schedules, and anecdotal records.

- Plan to assess every other response (e.g., odd numbered or even numbered items) on activities with multiple examples of similar tasks or problems.

- Use a scoring key and have students score their own work.

- Create portfolios and progress charts that allow students to complete selected recording tasks themselves.

Consider commercial, technology-based proficiency measures. Many textbooks are accompanied by proficiency measures, some of which may be completed by the student electronically. When this is appropriate and available, the computer maintains the scores and can generate many different types of data reports, including item analysis, progress reports, and so on.

USE ONE DATA SOURCE FOR DIFFERENT AUDIENCES

Paperwork is generated for many purposes, and it is sometimes helpful to examine the use of data in communicating with different audiences: parents, teachers, other professionals, and students. It is a useful exercise to think about how one could communicate with different audiences using one data source. One example would be to use curriculum-based assessment (CBA) for IEP evaluations and re-evaluations. Often, busy professionals grab a single measure, generally a standardized test, to assess students. But language in the IDEA reauthorization (Public Law 105-17, 1997) includes, "use a variety of assessment tools and strategies to gather relevant functional and developmental information" (20 U.S.C. § 1414 [b][2][A]), and "assessment tools and strategies that provide relevant information that directly assists persons in determining the educational needs of the child" (20 U.S.C. § 1414 [b][3][D]). CBA or criterion-referenced measures seem more in line with this directive and can also provide valuable information for instruction and monitoring student progress. Furthermore, if the CBA is done in areas of student need as described in IEP goals, the results would be appropriate for quarterly progress reports to parents and for communication with other professionals. That is four for the price of one — efficiency at its finest!

Clarifying Focus on the Student

When we refocus our attention on the needs of the students, we can make the most sense out of paperwork requirements. The time we invest in *planning* the instructional process will make time spent doing paperwork more meaningful. As special educators, we are professionals with expertise in and the primary responsibility for planning and delivering instruction to meet the unique learning needs of students with disabilities. Our commitment to students requires that we take the time to step back, reflect on their needs, and provide leadership in developing and implementing the instructional plan. The time we spend at the front end of the process will make time spent doing paperwork more meaningful.

COLLECT INFORMATION FOR MULTIPLE NEEDS

As we think about the student's needs, we can also be visualizing the nature of the information that will have to be collected and systematically maintained to monitor and report student progress. By planning up front, we can design strategies to collect information that will meet multiple needs. For example, are there similarities in the data needed to fulfill IEP data requirements and the data needed for quarterly progress reports or communication with other professionals? Is it possible that data collected for local progress monitoring or assessment results can be used for these purposes?

PLAN PAPERWORK AROUND THE CURRICULUM

All instructional goals and objectives need to be developed and planned against another key reference point — the curriculum.

It is helpful to remember that all instructional goals and objectives need to be developed and planned against another key reference point — the curriculum. Most typically, this will be the general education curriculum, unless an approved alternative curriculum has been agreed upon. In making decisions about curriculum, teachers analyze each student's information in order to identify his or her instructional needs. Frequently, when the general education curriculum is the referent for planning, proficiency measures and monitoring forms are available through the district. It is advisable to use these when available in order to save time and maintain a closer alignment with general education frameworks and practices.

Maintaining Focus on the Student

"When is the IEP due?" That seems to be the question many educators ask in order to determine how and when to begin drafting the document. With so many demands on teacher time, it is easy to understand why the IEP is seen as an additional burden and is relegated to the list of last minute tasks to squeeze into an already crowded calendar. What if we did not wait until the IEPs were due but worked on them all year long? What could be worse, you might ask! But hear us out. What if the IEP were incorporated into lesson planning so that students could take an active role in developing and monitoring their own educational programs? That is just what the National Information Center for Children and Youth with Disabilities (NICHCY) and others are advocating as a means for developing students' skills such as self-determination, awareness, and advocacy. And it is also what we are suggesting as a means to ensure that we remain focused on the student while maintaining legally compliant documents.

INVOLVE STUDENTS IN THEIR OWN IEP PLANNING

There are a variety of ways students can participate in the IEP process, but of course the format and procedure will need to be tailored to a student's age and degree of disability. NICHCY (2002) has published activities, audiotapes and workbooks to encourage collaboration between teachers and older students with disabilities. "A Student's Guide to the IEP" (http://www.nichcy. org/pubs/stguide/st1book.htm) provides step-by-step guidelines for walking students through the process of writing their own IEPs. In general, the idea is to begin the process of IEP planning at the beginning of the year. After discussing what an IEP is and some of the language that is used, older students may participate in reviewing their own IEP. It is a good idea to discuss key ideas with them, such as what the general education curriculum is or terms such as *present level of performance* and *accommodations*. With students who are able, we can take it a step further by having them revisit their IEPs periodically to provide feedback based on guided discussions. Sample questions for these discussions include:

- Are there goals, objectives, or benchmarks that students have met that need to be updated?

- Are there other goals or objectives that the student would like to address?

- Is the student able to recognize the connections between goals and objectives or benchmarks and his or her work in school?

This process may take the form of class discussions, individual seatwork, one-on-one conferences with the teacher and/or paraeducator, and even homework with parental support. Then, when it comes time for an annual review, the teacher can draft various sections of the IEP using data gathered throughout the year, rather than making a last minute dash to the deadline. In all of this, privacy issues and age appropriateness play a major role; and, as always, it is a good idea to inform parents of the plan and include them in the process if they are able to participate.

Be creative in involving students in their own IEPs. Now with a handle on writing on IEPs, what about using them to inform teaching and students' learning? Beyond self-assessment and reflection, how can we make students and parents active participants in implementing the IEP? First and foremost, it is important to make the information easily accessible to ourselves and other interested parties. A stack of twenty-page IEPs stored in a file cabinet is formidable even for those whose classes are not overflowing with students. Turning these legal documents into instructional tools is easier than you might think.

The idea is to turn the data-driven content of the IEP into manageable tools for instruction.

Some teachers have chosen to enlist their students in creating "IEP rings" that allow teachers, aides, and students to flip through the goals/objectives/benchmarks written as individual sentence strips several times daily. Again, do not panic! You may not need to create these rings yourself. Are the students able to assist? If so, it is a great activity for familiarizing them with the goals for teaching and learning. For younger students or those with more severe disabilities, find out whether parents are able to help. Parents benefit from familiarizing themselves with the skills their child is learning and can choose to provide reinforcement at home. Is the idea of a ring of IEP goals/objectives/benchmarks too daunting? If so, follow the lead of other teachers who have created subject-specific bookmarks listing only the two or three relevant goals/objectives/benchmarks. Students with reading and language arts goals create bookmarks that serve the dual purpose of keeping their page and keeping their attention on the overall goal at hand. The same principle can be used for math and written language goals. The idea is to turn the data-driven content of the IEP into manageable tools for instruction. It can actually be fun and easy to design these or similar tools, and the benefits extend to both you and your students.

Using Software Tailored to Special Education

So, we are off to the races and looking forward to sharing the IEP process with students and parents. What other strategies are available for monitoring and documenting student data, including strategies appropriate for young students or those with more severe disabilities? A simple, but underutilized solution is to create or adopt standardized reporting forms that you share or discover on the Internet. Using standard forms will allow you to systematize the information in a format easily accessible by yourself and others. You may choose to use forms adopted by your school or district or create your own.

There are a wide variety of educational forms created by and for teachers that are available online. Colleen Gallagher, a resource room teacher, created a recording sheet to be used by paraeducators so that they can collect data on student goals (http://www.teachertools.org/forms_dynam.asp). Teachers might choose to use this single form (a) to provide instructions for paraeducators when working with students, (b) as a quick reference of daily or weekly monitoring of student progress, and (c) as a reference when updating IEP goals. Figure 2 is just one example of how sharing the workload with other professionals can ease the paperwork burden and how the same source of data can be used for several purposes.

This and literally hundreds of other templates for teachers can be found at Education World (http://www.education-world.com/a_tech/tech101.

Figure 2. IEP Paraeducator Data Form

PROGRESS REPORT CHART FOR TELLING TIME

Goal: _____ will tell time (a) to the nearest hour and half hour, and (b) in increments of five minutes.

Target for Mastery: We will work on (a) this year and go on to (b) if (a) is met.

Suggested Activities: After you have helped the student in class, go over the time problem packet in the student's folder. Use time flash cards or a play clock and set it to a given time.

Chart Monthly Progress: Test goals (a) and (b) by giving the student a worksheet or having him or her set a clock for a series of given times. Use the form below to record numerical results and your notes.

TELLING TIME: MONTHLY PROGRESS CHART		
Date	Numerical Results How many times did the student give you the correct time when asked? (Express your answer as a ratio: 5/5, 7/10, etc.)	Notes

shtml) including homework notification for parents, notes for substitutes, IEP progress report forms, and IEP schedules. Another online resource for forms and letters is the template collection available with Microsoft Office Teacher Tools Download Center. Go to http://office.microsoft.com/templates and under "Browse Templates," click on "Education."

How else can technology be used to ease the demands of communication and record keeping? One strategy is to take advantage of new web-based applications and services applicable for special education. Although some require adoption by the school district (e.g., http://www.eSped.com),

Using Web-based IEPs allows for input from multiple participants without some of the constraints of geographical location.

others can be used in-house to assist with IEPs and administrative duties. Green (2000) in "Taming the Paper Tiger" presents a novel idea for managing paperwork: a district-wide networking system that creates paperless IEPs and allows individuals to submit student information from anywhere in the district. Other districts have taken this a step further by creating electronic templates and databases allowing the user to access and transfer existing information when developing an IEP. Using Web-based IEPs allows for input from multiple participants without some of the constraints of geographical location. In addition, commercial language conversion software often makes it possible to share print-outs of the IEP in English or Spanish. Teacher's Choice (http://www.db-es.com/), developed by db Education Solutions, is an example of IEP software designed to assist teachers in organizing and managing special education paperwork. Hailed as a timesaver and more effective than traditional paperwork, this is just one of the many software programs being developed to address the increasing demands placed on teachers for documentation.

Use the Web to keep all participants informed and involved. Connecting with parents and other professionals is often easier via the Internet and is a potential time saver. Involving parents and professionals in the IEP process by sharing drafts of an IEP before the meeting can ensure best services for students as well as saving time by allowing all parties to come to the meeting prepared. You can use free Web-based services (e.g., http://www.Gradeworks.com/) that allow teachers to post grades, assignments, contact information, calendars, and class activities on the Web, thereby promoting communication with parents and students and providing easy access to important information. Web-based services are also available for creating class calendars (http://www.calendarserver.com/) that display important dates, including parent conferences, standardized testing days, and grading periods. In some states, online networks have linked teachers from across districts to form online learning communities.

Conclusion

The special education profession, like the field of education itself, is undergoing continuous change from transformations in service delivery options to program requirements and accountability measures. However, what links past, present, and future educational reforms for most special educators is the student with special learning needs. More than likely, paperwork will always be part of the process; but it doesn't have to be done at the expense of best practices or quality instructional time. Paperwork is often a proxy for other challenging activities such as collaborating with colleagues and designing and delivering student-centered instruction. Federal and state governing bodies, as well as professional associations, are engaged in the paperwork debate: How much is enough? How much until it becomes counterproductive? It seems that although the length and content of the IEP continue to change, the intent of the document — to provide a written individualized educational program that holds schools accountable for serving students with special needs — will remain.

It is this focus on the student, along with reasonable accommodations, such as hiring clerical support, that will provide us with the correct direction for tackling paperwork requirements. In the face of competing demands, it is sometimes difficult to maintain a focus on serving students, but it is this focus that infuses meaning in the paperwork we do. A student-centered approach to assessing, planning, implementing, and documenting instruction and services may take the shape of informal communication with parents or formal documentation on an IEP. But one thing is clear: We must find and use available techniques that make paperwork work for us. Only then will it benefit our most important clients — our students.

It is this focus on the student that provides us the correct direction for tackling paperwork requirements.

References

Council for Exceptional Children. (2003). *What every special educator must know: Ethics, standards, and guidelines for special educators.* (5th ed., p.1). Arlington, VA: Author.

Green, M. Y. (2000, November). Taming the paper tiger. *NEA Today Online,* Cover Story. Retrieved October 11, 2002, from http:// www.nea.org/neatoday/0011/cover.html

Holcomb, S., Amundson, E., & Ralabate, P. (2000). *The new IDEA survival guide.* Annapolis Junction, MD: National Education Association.

Individuals With Disabilities Education Act, Amendment, Public Law 105-17 (1977), 20 U.S.C. § 1414, (2)(A) *et seq.*

Kronowitz, E. L. (1992). *Your first year of teaching.* (2nd ed.). White Plains, NY: Longman.

National Information Center for Children and Youth With Disabilities. (2002). *Helping students develop their IEPs* (2nd ed.). Technical Assistance Guide 2. Retrieved December 30, 2002, from http:/nichcy.org/pubs/stuguide/ta2book.htm

Parks, B. (n.d.). Seven time-management sanity savers. *Instructor.* Retrieved October 9, 2002, from http://teacher.scholastic.com/professional/classmgmt/timemanage.htm

Smith, B. A. (2000). Quantity matters: Annual instructional time in an urban school system. *Educational Administration Quarterly, 36*(5, Supplement), 652-683.

Tye, B., & O'Brien, L. (2002). Why are experienced teachers leaving the profession? *Phi Delta Kappan, 84*(1), 24-33.

**Chapter
6**

The View from the Top of
the Mountain

CASSANDRA PETERS-JOHNSON
DISTRICT OF COLUMBIA PUBLIC SCHOOLS

Teachers who are experienced and thriving have told us over and over
again in focus groups held by the Council for Exceptional Children that certain types of extracurricular activities help them to relieve stress. These activities include reading, researching, and presenting information about their
profession; training and mentoring others; and making contacts in distant
geographic locations, especially in other school districts. We could not imagine how taking on additional activities could *relieve* stress rather than adding
to it in a job that is as time-consuming and demanding as special education.

But the teachers also told us *why* the additional activities had this effect:
By interacting with other teachers, they learned new ways to get things
done, assessed their standing in relation to their colleagues in the field,
increased their self-confidence, and generally helped themselves to develop

a long-term, holistic, overall perspective from the top of the mountain. Only from the mountaintop could these teachers become actively involved as leaders in changing and improving their careers, their districts, and the profession of special education. Their involvement contributed as much to the satisfaction and enjoyment they experienced in their lives and careers as it contributed to the circles around them.

The preceding chapters of this book have described many strategies that will help you thrive in the profession you have chosen. Here are five final pointers that will further enhance your enjoyment of a thriving career.

Share Your Thoughts and Ideas With Other Teachers

In Chapter Two, Teresa Zutter urged you to read about and keep up-to-date on the issues affecting your school district's administration and its leaders. Keeping informed also allows you to explore, investigate, and develop your own thoughts and opinions, and it can lead to fresh ideas about how to approach the issues that arise in your classroom and school. Be one of those people who knows where she stands on the issues from an informed point of view. Read, attend meetings, and make friends of other educators whenever you have the opportunity.

Discuss what you've learned. When you discuss your ideas with trusted others, you also develop a better awareness of where you stand in relation to them. You can learn from their views. You become more sure of yourself and more confident as you think through issues and express your own thoughts and perspectives.

Learn About Other States, Districts, Jobs, and Situations

As you expand your boundaries in meetings and through contacts with educators from different districts and states, compare the issues you face with those faced elsewhere. You will learn about a number of different ways that problems are approached and solved. This provides you with the potential to bring home new ideas and efficiencies that can be adapted to your own classroom, school, or district.

Learn about other positions and professions in order to develop a deeper understanding of their work, vocabulary, approaches, and attitudes.

Learn about other positions and professions in order to develop a deeper understanding of their work, their vocabulary, their approaches, and their attitudes. Include people in related educational and noneducational positions, such as other types of teachers, support staff, and school administrators. Also include contacts with professionals in other fields, such as counselors, therapists, and social workers. You will undoubtedly be called on frequently during your career to collaborate with professionals in these fields. This will be much easier if you have taken every opportunity to learn all you can about their work and have observed how you, as a special educator, are in a position to work effectively with them. Over time, you will develop a broader knowledge of the ways in which all things go together, a knowledge that can enhance your capacity as an educator and expand your contribution to your district. You will also gain the freedom and perspective that comes with a wide network of professional contacts.

Use Professional Contributions to Further Your Career

Sometimes it is extremely difficult to plan for and set aside the time to pay attention to your own thoughts! But if you succeed in scheduling a writing or speaking project, for example, you will force yourself to place a higher priority on your independent learning and professional development — in spite of the conflicting demands on your time. After you have thought through a topic or subject, it only takes a few minutes to write a two-paragraph proposal to present at a conference. Once your proposal is accepted, you will give precedence to further developing your concept and your presentation.

After you have thought through a topic or subject, it only takes a few minutes to write a two-paragraph proposal to present at a conference.

So speak, write, train! Share the insights you have developed from your contacts with people in other districts and professions. You will earn gratitude and admiration as you build a resume that enhances not only your teaching career but broadens your other professional options. An excellent way to examine in detail how you do your job is to become a mentor to newer teachers when offered the opportunity. Being a mentor gives you access to someone else's base of knowledge and to her fresh, new attitude. This is a perfect opportunity to review and analyze your experience and knowledge and find ways to apply it to others' teaching. As you understand their learning processes, you will gain the ability to describe your unique style as a special educator. Know that while you learn and share, you are also contributing to the growth of your profession.

Recognize That You Are Truly Making a Difference to Your Students, to Our Culture and Society, and to the Future

It is easy to forget in the hubbub of day-to-day activity that you should never take your contributions for granted. Appreciate your professional growth every day. Remember how much your repertoire of teaching skills has increased since you were a new teacher, and appreciate the advancement in your knowledge and in your career over the years. Make note of the problems solved: Each year will present a new type of problem with new challenges.

As you thrive professionally, you will come to realize that you make a huge and tangible difference to the present and future lives of your students. This is a difference that can be measured in the achievement of goals and objectives that are documented and recognized from day to day, month to month, and year to year. Through documentation, you can know for a fact that your students are progressing. By teaching your students the philosophies and skills that our society values, you are strengthening our culture and our society, as well as our future. Keep that in mind: It will give you the confidence you need to keep taking your own steps forward.

One Last Pointer

Network with your peers and other professionals, and maintain that sense of personal and professional renewal that is so important to thriving.

As the other authors of *Thriving as a Special Educator* have suggested, we can't stress enough the importance of furthering your professional education. This is your key to staying connected with the latest information. Network with your peers and other professionals, and maintain that sense of personal and professional renewal that is so important to thriving. There are many professional development opportunities available through your school district or your professional organization. What you choose to study further is up to you, but do choose something, and pursue it as often as you can. Annual conventions of your state or national association are a great place to explore a wealth of topics — or to focus on one particular area. And don't forget the wealth of information to be mined as you delve more deeply into your specialty area and attend workshops, institutes, Web seminars, and online courses. You'll be glad you did!